Active Learning Across the Curriculum

Teaching the Way They Learn

3rd edition

**More than 300 games and activities
to bring learning to life!**

Rae Pica

DEDICATION

This book is dedicated to all of the early childhood professionals who, despite policies that discourage active learning, understand the mind/body connection and continue to teach children in developmentally appropriate ways!

Contents

Introduction • x

Section One: Art / 1

Unit 1:   **Spatial Relationships • 3**

Personal Space / 4
You Can Take It with You / 6
Follow the Leader / 8

Unit 2:   **Shape & Size • 10**

Mirror, Mirror / 11
I Spy... / 13
Show Me... / 15

Unit 3: Line • 17

What's My Line? / 18
Up and Down, Side to Side, and Corner to Corner / 20
Drop Me a Line / 22

Unit 4:   **Color • 24**

What Am I? / 25
Color Me... / 27
Primary Colors / 29

Unit 5: Texture • 31

Soft and Hard / 32
Smooth and Rough / 34
Feathers and Seashells and Bears, Oh My / 36

Section Two: Language Arts / 38

Unit 6: **Listening • 39**

Listen Up! / 40
Get into Action / 42
How Many Sounds? / 44
What's That Sound? / 45

Unit 7: **Speaking • 46**

What's in a Name? /47
Tell Me About... / 49
Four Voices / 51

Unit 8: **Reading • 53**

Action! / 54
Descriptive Words / 56
Happy Endings / 58

Unit 9: **Writing • 59**

Left to Right /60
Show Me the Letter... / 62
Skywriting / 64

Section Three: Mathematics / 66

Unit 10: **Quantitative and Positional Concepts • 68**

The Long and Short of It / 69
Light and Heavy / 71
One More Time / 73
Me and My Shadow / 75
Over the River and Through the Woods / 77

Unit 11: **Number Awareness and Recognition • 79**

Number Shapes I / 80
Number shapes II / 82
Invisible Numbers / 84

Unit 12:   **Counting • 86**

Blast Off! / 87
How Many Parts? / 89
Oh, the Possibilities / 91

Unit 13:   **Basic Geometry • 93**

Line 'Em Up / 94
On the Right Path / 96
Right to the Point / 98
What a Square! / 99

Unit 14:   **Simple Computation • 101**

"Roll Over" / 102
Add 'Em and Subtract 'Em / 105
How Many Parts Now? / 107

Section Four: Music / 109

Unit 15:   **Tempo • 111**

Moving Slow/Moving Fast / 112
Moving Slow/Moving Fast – Again / 114
Slow to Fast and Back Again / 116

Unit 16:   **Volume • 118**

Moving Softly/Moving Loudly / 119
Moving Softly/Moving Loudly – Again / 121
Soft to Loud and Back Again / 123

Unit 17:   **Staccato and Legato • 125**

"Pop Goes the Weasel" / 126
Statues / 128
Bound and Free / 130

Unit 18:   **Pitch • 132**

Do-Re-Mi / 133
High and Low / 135

Moving High/Moving Low / 137

Unit 19:   **Mood • 139**

In a Mellow Mood / 140
What Mood Are You In? / 142
In the Mood / 144

Unit 20:   **Rhythm • 146**

Body Rhythm / 147
Match the Movement / 149
Echo / 151
Common Meters / 153

Section Five: Science / 155

Unit 21:   **My Body • 156**

Simon Says / 157
Hands Down / 159
Move It! / 161
Common Senses / 163
A Breath of Fresh Air / 165

Unit 22:   **Hygiene • 167**

Rub-a-Dub-Dub / 168
Hair Care / 170
A Bite Out of Life / 172
Laundry Day / 174

Unit 23:   **Nutrition • 176**

Eat Your Fruits and Veggies / 177
Get Ready, Spaghetti! / 179
Bread, Bread, Bread / 181

Unit 24:   **Seasons • 183**

Autumn / 184
Winter / 186
Spring / 188

Summer / 190

Unit 25:   **Animals • 192**

My Favorite Animal / 193
Rabbits and 'Roos / 195
Giddy-Up / 197
Creep-Crawly / 199
Ducks, Cows, Cats, and Dogs / 201

Unit 26:   **Simple Science • 203**

Floating on Air / 204
May the Force Be with You / 206
It's Electric! / 208
Balancing Act / 210
The Machine / 212
It's Magnetic! / 214

Section Six: Social Studies / 216

Unit 27:   **Self-Concept • 217**

"If You're Happy" / 218
Oh, What a Feeling / 220
"Punchinello" / 221

Unit 28:   **Families and Friends • 223**

This Is My Friend / 224
All in the Family / 226
Palm to Palm / 228
Musical Hoops / 230
It Takes Two / 232

Unit 29:   **Holidays and Celebrations • 234**

Pass the Present / 235
Light the Candles / 237
Let's Hear It for the USA / 239

Unit 30:   **Occupations • 242**

"This Is the Way We..." / 242
Equal Opportunity / 244
Makin' Music / 246
Keepin' House / 248

Unit 31:   **Transportation • 250**

"Row, Row, Row Your Boat" / 251
Traffic Lights / 253
All Aboard! / 255
By Air of By Sea / 257

About the Author / 259

Introduction

"If they can't learn the way we teach, maybe we should teach the way they learn."
Ignacio Estrada

Did you know that movement is a young child's preferred mode of learning?

When we think of the words *children* and *movement*, physical development is typically the first benefit to come to mind. We might even associate movement, so closely related to play, with children's social development. But people seldom link it in their minds with cognitive development. And that's a shame because young children learn best when they physically experience concepts.

As Confucius said, "What I hear, I forget. What I see, I remember. What I do, I know." Since then, we've discovered that most people are more likely to really *know* what they have a chance to *do*. In fact, research has shown us that the more senses involved in the learning process, the greater the impression it makes and the longer it stays with us.

Children come to us as thinking, feeling, *moving* human beings; yet in too many classrooms they're treated as though they exist only from the neck up. The belief that sitting equals learning is a wrong-headed one and must be squashed!

Consider the following: When children move over, under, around, through, beside, and near objects and others, they better grasp the meaning of these prepositions and geometry concepts. When they perform a "slow walk" or skip "lightly," adjectives and adverbs become much more than abstract ideas. When they're given the opportunity to physically demonstrate such action words as *stomp, pounce, stalk,* or *slither* – or descriptive words such as *smooth, strong, gentle,* or *enormous* – word comprehension is immediate and long-lasting. The words are in context, as opposed to being a mere collection of letters. This is what promotes emergent literacy and a love of language.

Similarly, if children take on high, low, wide, and narrow body shapes, they'll have a much greater understanding of these quantitative concepts – and opposites – than do children who are merely presented with the words and their definitions. When they act out the lyrics to "Roll Over," they can see that five minus one leaves four. The same understanding – and fascination – results when children have personal experience with such scientific concepts as gravity, flotation, evaporation, magnetics, balance and stability, and action and reaction.

Noted educator and author Eric Jensen labels these kinds of learning experiences as *implicit* – like learning to ride a bike. At the other end of the continuum is *explicit* learning – such as being told the capital of Peru. He asks, If you hadn't ridden a bike in five years, would you still be able to do it? And, If you hadn't heard the capital for Peru for five years, would you still remember what it was? Explicit learning may get the facts across more quickly than learning through exploration and discovery, but the latter has far more meaning to children and stays with them longer.

Yet another benefit of active learning is that it provides you with an effective means of evaluation. The traditional question-and-answer method doesn't always reveal students who have failed to grasp the concept being discussed, but movement experiences allow a teacher to immediately detect those students who don't understand.

Finally, there is one more – very important – reason why active learning is more effective than the kind that takes place in a seat: as mentioned, it's the young child's favorite mode of learning. Why would we want to teach them in any way that isn't their preference?

About This Book

Typically, the early childhood curriculum consists of six major content areas, in addition to physical education (movement): art, language arts, mathematics, music, science, and social studies. This book, therefore, is divided into six sections – one for each content area. These appear in alphabetical order, so as not to give the impression that one content area is more or less important than another.

Each section is introduced with a brief discussion about the content area and its connection to movement. I hope that these introductions will help you look at traditional content areas in a whole new light – not just as subjects to be taught but as *potential* – for exploration and discovery, for new ways to bring enthusiasm to the classroom, and for new ideas that help keep you excited about teaching.

Following the introduction to each content area are the lesson plans. Each offers learning objectives ("What it Teaches"); a list of equipment or props required or suggested ("What You'll Need"); the principal activity ("What to Do"); teaching hints ("How to Ensure Success"); possible extensions, variations, and/or alternatives ("What Else You Can Do"); and examples of how the activity and extensions connect with other content areas ("More Curriculum Connectors"). At the end of each lesson plan is a section titled "What Else I Did." This part has been left blank to allow you to jot down other ideas you (or the children) had while working with the activities, other "connections" made, or notes regarding what worked and what bears repeating.

The lesson plans are organized around topics falling under the major content areas. In the cases of science and social studies, the topics are often themes commonly explored in early childhood classrooms and centers. Because language arts encompass listening, speaking, reading, and writing, the language arts section has been divided into those four topics. The remaining content areas – art, mathematics, and music – are organized according to those concepts suitable for exploration with children ages 4 to 8. Every topic has three to six lesson plans, arranged from least to most challenging.

The activities are not entirely original in nature (there's much truth in the old adage that "There's nothing new under the sun"). Rather, several stem from tried and tested activities that have been delighting children for years.

Because outdoor play is so critical to children's development – and children seem to be spending less and less time outside these days – where appropriate, I've added specific suggestions for how some of the activities can be conducted in outdoor settings. In some cases, taking the activity outside impacts the way in which it's conducted, or affects the learning outcomes for the children. In other cases, the only change is that the activity is taking place in a different setting. It's my hope, however, that by suggesting the possibility, I'll remind you of the potential of the outdoors as a setting for learning.

Every effort has been made to require as few props as possible. This serves three purposes: (1) to make it easier for you, (2) to ensure that these activities can be a part of *every* program, and (3) to provide opportunities for the children to use their *body* as a tool for learning. My philosophy has always been that the only absolutely necessary piece of equipment required for movement is the child's body.

How to Use This Book

These activities are designed to be used with children ages 4 to 8. I have assigned no specific ages to each lesson plan, because they are meant to be explored as the children are *developmentally* ready. I have, however, arranged them in order from least to most challenging within each topic. Also, whenever applicable, the topics within each content area are similarly arranged. Further, you often will find suggestions for making an activity less or more challenging, under "How to Ensure Success" and "What Else You Can Do."

You know the children well and, therefore, are the best judge of what they are or are not capable of. Trust your judgment. If you try an activity and find that the children aren't ready for it, consider it a valuable learning experience – and try again at a later time.

As you know, not all children learn in the same way. So talk to the children about the concept, demonstrate when applicable, and provide opportunities for the children to touch if appropriate. This approach engages multiple senses.

Whenever possible, participation in these games and activities shouldn't be isolated events. They should be connected, as much as possible, to the daily curriculum. For example, the lesson plan calling for exploration of descriptive words (under "Language Arts") doesn't have to use an arbitrary list of descriptive words. Rather, if you've just read a story to the children, in which there were a lot of descriptive words, you could then use those words as impetus for the movement activity. As another example, you could use the activities under "Art" in conjunction with specific art projects – for instance, a project relating to shape or color. You can also excerpt and incorporate the activities within each lesson plan.

Movement makes its greatest impact as a tool for learning when it is used together with other approaches. As with any aspect of early childhood education, young children do not learn best when subjects are segregated. (Content areas are separated in this book for the sake of organization.)

Other occasions when you might refer to this book include:
- when the children have been sitting too long and need an opportunity to move;
- when you want a transitional activity;
- when the children just aren't "getting it" through other teaching methods;
- when you and/or the children are in need of something new – and fun – to do; and
- when you want to help parents and others understand why movement and active learning are essential to the early childhood curriculum.

Remember, every teacher and every child brings new ideas and new potential to the concept of active learning. Use these activities – as well as those they're sure to inspire – to enhance learning, develop rapport among the children, gain immediate feedback on learning, promote a positive attitude toward education that can influence future learning and, above all, to educate the whole child!

Section One

ART

Art and movement have a number of things in common – particularly when young children are concerned. Because it involves movement, art helps develop motor skills. **Gross motor skills**[1] are used in art activities such as painting on an easel, creating murals, body tracing, and working with clay. Children use **fine motor control**[2], which is refined later than gross motor control, during art activities such as working with small paintbrushes, cutting with scissors, and pasting. Both art and movement also help develop eye-hand coordination.

But perhaps the most significant common factor between art and movement is that they both promote self-expression. When given ample opportunity to explore possibilities – whether through movement or a variety of art materials – children make nonverbal statements about who they are and what is important to them. Through both mediums they can express emotions, work out their concerns, and achieve the satisfaction that comes from success. These results can occur only when the child's movements and artwork aren't censored by adults and when their responses are accepted and valued as evidence of the child's individuality. With acceptance, children gain confidence in their abilities to express themselves, solve problems, and reveal their creativity.

Finally, such concepts as shape, size, spatial relationships, and line are part of both art and movement education. Thus, whenever children arrange their bodies in the space around them, they're exploring artistic as well as physical concepts. With their bodies, they're creating lines and shapes. When they move into different levels, in different directions, along different pathways, and in relation to others and to objects, they're increasing their spatial

---

[1] **gross motor skills** Movements, such as running and jumping, that use the large muscles.
[2] **fine motor control** Development of skills using small muscles, such as writing and using scissors.

awareness. Yet, even artistic concepts such as color and texture can be explored and expressed through movement.

Unit 1
Spatial Relationships

Personal Space

What It Teaches
- ✓ The concept of **personal space**[3]
- ✓ Respect for others' personal space

What You'll Need
- ✓ Carpet squares or plastic hoops (optional)
- ✓ "New Age" (preferably nonrhythmic) music (optional)

What to Do
- ✓ Have each child find a spot to stand, far enough away from each other so they can stretch out their arms without touching anyone else.
- ✓ Ask them to reach their arms as high, low, and wide as they can without moving from their spots. Challenge them to explore all the space around their bodies. How high can they get? How low? Have they checked out the area in between? What other body parts can they explore with?
- ✓ Explain that they've just explored their very own personal space and it's a lot like being inside a giant bubble!

How to Ensure Success
Some children require tangible evidence of personal space. Provide carpet squares or hoops if you think they'll be helpful. Ask the children to imagine they're each on their own little island.

What Else You Can Do
- ✓ To grant the children even more ownership of their personal spaces – and to stimulate the imagination – ask them to pretend to paint the insides of their spaces. They can decorate with stripes or polka dots and with any colors they want.
- ✓ Challenge the children to discover how many ways they can move with their feet "glued" to the floor. After a while, allow them to "unglue" one foot and, finally, both. (Remind them that they must still stay in their personal spaces.)

---

[3]**personal space**   The area immediately surrounding the body and including whatever the person can reach while remaining in one spot.

More Curriculum Connectors

✓ Self-concept, which is explored through the idea of personal space, is the beginning of *social studies* for young children.

✓ To make *language arts* part of the process, ask the children to describe how they've decorated their personal spaces.

✓ Play "New Age" *music* in the background as the children are creating their spaces.

✓ The quantitative concepts of high, low, and wide art part of *mathematics*.

What Else I Did

_____

_____

_____

_____

_____

_____

_____

_____

_____

What It Teaches
- ✓ The concepts of personal and **general space**[4]
- ✓ Respect for others' space

What You'll Need
- ✓ One plastic hoop per child, if possible

What to Do
- ✓ Once the children understand the idea of personal space, explain that personal space goes with us wherever we go.
- ✓ If you have enough hoops for everyone, hand them out and ask the children to each step inside one, lifting it to the waist. (If you don't have hoops, ask the children to reach out their arms to the sides.)
- ✓ Challenge the children to walk all around the room without letting their hoops (or hands) touch anyone else's.
- ✓ Once they're succeeding with this, increase the challenge by asking them to vary their speed or to move backward or sideward.

How to Ensure Success
Use the image of cars moving safely in heavy traffic to encourage the children not to touch one another.

Begin simply, with the children moving forward, along straight pathways. Wait until they've mastered this before asking them to try other directions as well as curving and zigzagging pathways.

What Else You Can Do
- ✓ When your children demonstrate that they can respect one another's personal space, they're ready to play Shrinking Room (or Shrinking Space, if you play it outside). In this game, stand with your arms and legs outstretched, pretending to be a wall. Begin at one end of the room, allowing the children the maximum amount of space in which to move without touching one another. Then take a big step forward, thereby decreasing the size of the room (and the allowable space in which to move). Continue gradually reducing the size of the room, and stop while the children are still able to succeed.

More Curriculum Connectors
- ✓ Respecting the personal space of others is an aspect of *social studies*.

---

[4] **general space**   The space shared by all, which usually is limited only by walls, floor, and ceilings.

✓ Gradually reducing the size of the room can be a general lesson in *mathematics*.

What Else I Did

_____
_____
_____
_____
_____
_____
_____
_____

Follow the Leader

What It Teaches
- ✓ The concept of general space
- ✓ **Visual discrimination** [5]
- ✓ The ability to physically replicate what the eyes see
- ✓ Practice with locomotor skills

What You'll Need
No equipment or materials needed

What to Do
- ✓ Play the traditional game of Follow the Leader, making sure to include lots of variety in levels, pathways, directions, and locomotor skills. For example, you can move on tiptoe or as small as you can be (levels); forward, backward, and sideward (directions); in straight, curving, circular, and zigzagging pathways. Use any form of locomotion the children can execute successfully (walking, running, galloping, leaping, etc.).

How to Ensure Success
Start off slowly, with the simplest examples for the children to follow.

At first, don't often change what you're doing. Give the children a lot of opportunity to follow you before you modify the challenge.

Make sure that all the children can see you!

What Else You Can Do
- ✓ Play this game outdoors, where there's more space and a variety of obstacles not found indoors, and you can put a whole new spin on it!
- ✓ When the children are ready for the challenge, explore the concepts of *accelerando* (gradual increase in tempo, or speed) and *ritardando* (gradual decrease in speed). Start – and end – with a very slow walk, exploring the full range from very slow to very fast.
- ✓ When the children are developmentally ready to act as leaders, modify the game. Begin as usual, but after a few minutes, call out the name of one of the children. That child breaks off from the line, with everybody behind him or her following that child instead of you. Continue to do this until you have several small lines moving throughout the room. Occasionally call out "Switch," indicating that the child in front of the line should move to the back, and, in doing so, create a new leader.

---

[5] **visual discrimination** The ability to distinguish among things seen.

More Curriculum Connectors

- ✓ The cooperation involved in this activity is a lesson in *social studies*.
- ✓ Being able to physically replicate what the eyes see is necessary in writing, part of *language arts*.
- ✓ In the extension activity, you can count the number of children in each of the lines, a *mathematics* exercise.
- ✓ Accelerando and ritardando are *musical* concepts.

What Else I Did

_____
_____
_____
_____
_____
_____
_____
_____
_____

Unit 2

Shape and Size

What It Teaches
- ✓ Shape awareness
- ✓ Visual discrimination
- ✓ Ability to physically replicate what the eyes see

What You'll Need
No equipment or materials needed

What to Do
- ✓ Talk to the children about how mirrors work. Where in their homes do they have mirrors?
- ✓ Explain that you're going to stand in front of them and they should pretend they're your mirror reflection – doing what you do and resembling you as closely as possible.
- ✓ Create various shapes with your body at different levels in space. Possibilities include round, straight, wide, narrow, and pointed.

How to Ensure Success
At first, move slowly from one position to another, using as few body parts as possible (for example, just the arms, instead of an arm and a leg).

Begin with the simplest shapes. When the children are developmentally ready, include more difficult shapes, such as crooked, angular, or oval.

Explore symmetrical shapes before you begin demonstrating asymmetrical ones.

What Else You Can Do
- ✓ When the children no longer need you to demonstrate, ask them to show you body shapes that are round, straight, wide, narrow, etc.
- ✓ When the children are ready to cooperate with partners, have them pair off and play a mirror game in twos, in which the partners take turns initiating and imitating.

More Curriculum Connectors

- ✓ The concept of mirror reflection relates to *science*.
- ✓ Shape is also part of geometry, which is part of *mathematics*.
- ✓ Being able to physically replicate what the eyes see is a necessary part of learning to write, which falls under the heading of *language arts*. Read and discuss *No Mirrors in My Nana's House*, by Ysaye M. Barnwell.
- ✓ Cooperating with a partner relates to *social studies*.

What Else I Did

_____

_____

_____

_____

_____

_____

_____

_____

_____

I Spy...

What It Teaches
✓ Shape awareness
✓ Visual discrimination
✓ Ability to physically replicate what the eyes see

What You'll Need
✓ Objects typically found in a classroom
✓ Pictures or actual examples of teapots

What to Do
✓ Point out objects of fairly simple shape throughout the room, discussing the various shapes with the children. Possible objects might include a desk, chair, chalkboard, rug, stuffed animal, piece of chalk, piece of paper, etc.
✓ Invite the children to take on the shapes of these objects with their body or body parts.

How to Ensure Success
Discuss one object at a time, and then ask the children to take on its shape while the description is still fresh in their mind.

Use simple descriptions with the children, such as *flat* or *round*, *long* or *short*. It's best to first ask the children for their descriptions. Then, if they need more direction, specifically ask if an object is flat or round, etc.

Refine the responses with follow-up questions and challenges. For example, if a child depicts the roundness of a rug but not the flatness, you might ask if he or she can get as close to the floor as a rug.

What Else You Can Do
✓ Show the children pictures or actual examples of teapots of different shapes and sizes. Then sing "I'm a Little Teapot." Encourage a variety of responses.
✓ Chant "I spy with my little eye something in the room that's long and straight (short and round, very crooked, etc.) ..." Have the children look around, determine what it could be, and take on the shape themselves. (It's best if each challenge has more than one response.) The children then can tell you what object they've chosen to depict.
✓ Play I Spy outdoors to open up many new possibilities.

More Curriculum Connectors
✓ Shape is an aspect of geometry, which is part of *mathematics*. Introduce the children to

Tana Hoban's book, *Shapes, Shapes, Shapes.*

✓ Being able to physically replicate what the eyes see if a necessary part of learning to write, which is an element of *language arts*, as is describing the shapes. You can incorporate Dayle Ann Dodds' book, *The Shape of Things*, into your lesson.

✓ Singing "I'm a Little Teapot" brings *music* into the mix.

What Else I Did

_____
_____
_____
_____
_____
_____
_____
_____

What It Teaches
- ✓ Awareness of shape and size
- ✓ Comparisons
- ✓ An introduction to suffixes

What You'll Need
No equipment or materials needed

What to Do
- ✓ Ask the children to show you a big shape. Then challenge them to make it a little bigger and, finally, the biggest it can be.
- ✓ Continue with challenges such as *little, littler, littlest; round, rounder, roundest; long, longer, longest*; etc.

How to Ensure Success
At first, demonstrate this concept yourself.

Use objects such as straws to demonstrate the concept.

What Else You Can Do
- ✓ When the children are developmentally ready, divide the class into groups of three. Then challenge each group to illustrate, among themselves, some of the examples listed previously, as well as others.

More Curriculum Connectors
- ✓ Shape and size relate to *mathematics*, as does the concept of comparison. Introduce Tana Hoban's *Is It Larger? Is It Smaller?*
- ✓ Suffixes fall under the heading of *language arts*. The book *The Best Bug Parade* by Stuart J. Murphy is about size relationships.
- ✓ The cooperation required in the extension activity is part of *social studies*.

What Else I Did

_____
_____
_____
_____
_____
_____

Unit 3
Line

What It Teaches
- ✓ The concept of line
- ✓ Visual discrimination
- ✓ Ability to physically replicate what the eyes see

What You'll Need
Drawings or examples of straight, curving, and crooked lines

What to Do
- ✓ Show the children drawings or actual examples of lines that are straight, curving, and crooked. Can they describe what makes a line curving versus crooked?
- ✓ Ask them to show you, with their whole bodies, straight, curving, and crooked lines.
- ✓ Can they find at least two different body parts (e.g., arms, legs, fingers) with which to demonstrate straight, curving, and crooked lines?

How to Ensure Success
In the beginning, provide as much direct instruction (demonstration and imitation) as necessary.

Suggest *stretching* to ensure straightness, and *roundness* to encourage curves. This also might be an appropriate time to introduce the children to the word *angle* in relation to crooked lines.

What Else You Can Do
- ✓ Call out the words *straight, curving*, and *crooked* – at varying tempos and in various orders – challenging the children to match their body shape with the word called.
- ✓ Play Head, Bellies, Toes, in which you call out these body parts at varying tempos and in varying orders, with the children touching the body part(s) called. With this version, however, you can add the extra challenge of asking children to assume a straight body line while touching the head, a curving body line while touching the belly, and a crooked body line which touching the toes. (Substitute the word *tummies* for *bellies* if the children are more familiar with this term.)

More Curriculum Connectors
- ✓ Line is also part of basic geometry, so it falls under *mathematics*.
- ✓ Describing lines constitutes *language arts*. You also might read *When a Line Bends…A Shape Begins* by Rhonda Gowler Greene.
- ✓ Identifying body parts is basic *science*.

What Else I Did

_____

_____

_____

_____

_____

_____

_____

_____

Up and Down, Side to Side, and Corner to Corner

What It Teaches
- ✓ The concept of line
- ✓ Visual discrimination
- ✓ Ability to physically replicate what the eyes see

What You'll Need
- ✓ A jump rope, or something similar, for demonstration purposes

What to Do
- ✓ Introduce the concepts of *vertical*, *horizontal*, and *diagonal* by using the jump rope to demonstrate these kinds of lines for the children.
- ✓ As you demonstrate each of the preceding, challenge the children to show you the same kind of line with their bodies and, later, with body parts.

How to Ensure Success
At first you'll want to provide a constant visual demonstration for the children as they form the various lines with their bodies. In other words, if you're using a jump rope to demonstrate a line, hold it in position until the children have finished creating their shapes. (Later, you can demonstrate briefly and then challenge the children to replicate what they saw.)

What Else You Can Do
- ✓ Once the children have had a lot of experience with these types of lines, ask them to show you horizontal, vertical, and diagonal without any visual aids.
- ✓ Ask the children to "paint" imaginary lines of all kinds in the air – first with their hands and then with various other body parts – on the floor, with their feet. Can they do it with both left and right hands and feet? What colors do they imagine their lines to be?

More Curriculum Connectors
- ✓ Line is also part of simple geometry, or *mathematics*.
- ✓ Ask the children to identify which letters of the alphabet include horizontal, vertical, and diagonal lines, making *language arts* part of the project.

What Else I Did

_____

_____

_____

_____

_____

_____

_____

_____

Drop Me a Line

What It Teaches
- ✓ The concept of line
- ✓ Visual discrimination
- ✓ Pathways

What You'll Need
- ✓ Several jump ropes, or masking tape, to make visible pathways
- ✓ Materials for an obstacle course (optional)

What to Do
- ✓ Use jump ropes or masking tape to create a variety of lines on the floor. Be sure to include all lines the children have experienced to this point (straight, curving, crooked, horizontal, vertical, and diagonal).
- ✓ Acting as leader, play Follow the Leader with the children, following the pathways created by the rope or tape.
- ✓ Once the children are familiar with this activity, have them take turns acting as leader.

How to Ensure Success
Begin by simply walking along the created pathways. Later, you can try following them with other locomotor (traveling) skills (run, jump, leap, gallop, slide, skip).

Make each pathway as big or as long as possible so the children have a chance to fully experience them.

What Else You Can Do
- ✓ Bring the game outside, where there is a possibility of even longer pathways.
- ✓ Explore various elements of movement by leading or encouraging the children to move with varying amounts of force (tiptoeing or stomping, for instance), in different body shapes, or at different tempos (slowly and quickly).
- ✓ Make your lines part of an obstacle course that also includes tunnels (old tires and appliance boxes work just fine), objects to crawl and creep over and under, and obstacles to move around. (Obstacle courses are great outside, too.)

More Curriculum Connectors
- ✓ Line and positional concepts come under the heading of *mathematics*.
- ✓ Experimenting with different amounts of force falls under the heading of *science*, while tempo belongs to the content area of *music*.
- ✓ Follow the Leader is a cooperative activity, which makes it *social studies*.

What Else I Did

_____

_____

_____

_____

_____

_____

_____

_____

_____

Unit 4

Color

What Am I?

What It Teaches
✓ Color and shape awareness

What You'll Need
✓ Pictures or examples of objects in various colors

What to Do
✓ Show the children pictures or examples of objects in various colors – one at a time – and ask the children to demonstrate the shape of each object. Possibilities include a yellow banana, a green plant, a red apple, an orange, a bunch of purple grapes, or a white snowflake.

How to Ensure Success
Because the idea behind this activity is to associate certain colors with certain shapes, show the children objects that typically are one shape and one color. Examples: a *bowl* generally comes in one shape but could be any color. A banana has a particular shape and is most often yellow.

If necessary, provide additional guidance by talking about curves and straight lines, etc. At first you may want to demonstrate the shapes yourself.

What Else You Can Do
✓ Give the children an assortment of objects from which to choose. Then, have each child pick one and take on its shape. Ask the rest of the children to guess which object it is.
✓ Play What's Missing? with the objects. With this game, one child hides his eyes as another removes an object and places it behind her back. (All the children place their hands behind their back so the child guessing doesn't know who took it.) You then instruct the first child to open his eyes and ask him to guess what's missing. In this version, the child who is guessing should include the *color* of the object too.
✓ Use the children's book *Brown Bear, Brown Bear, What Do You See?* (written by Bill Martin, Jr. and illustrated by Eric Carle) to inspire a discussion of differently colored creatures, both real and imaginary (e.g., a green frog and a purple cat). Then invite the children to show you how some of these creatures *move*.

More Curriculum Connectors
✓ Identifying and sorting are part of both *mathematics* and *science*.
✓ The guessing games bring in *language arts*, as does the children's book.

What Else I Did

_____

_____

_____

_____

_____

_____

_____

_____

Color Me...

What It Teaches
✓ Color discrimination
✓ Self-expression

What You'll Need
✓ A variety of colors

What to Do
✓ Show the children assorted colors, one at a time, discussing what each reminds them of. Does the color bring certain objects, or perhaps creatures, to mind? Certain feelings?
✓ Again display each color one at a time, asking the children to show you *with their bodies* what the color brings to mind.

How to Ensure Success
Use only colors with which the children are very familiar – and have several possible associations – until they're ready for greater challenges. To begin, possibilities include red, blue, yellow, green, white, and black.

Be sure to validate all responses so the children understand that it's possible – and okay – to have different ideas. For example, the color blue would have a wide variety of meanings to the children; it could bring to mind the sky, water, feeling sad, or feeling cold, or it could conjure up an image you would never think of!

What Else You Can Do
✓ Assign small groups (or perhaps three children) to represent assorted colors. When you call out a group's color, those children each demonstrate what it means to them. The rest of the children can try to guess what the different responses represent.

More Curriculum Connectors
✓ Self-expression is an important part of early *social studies*. You also can incorporate multicultural education with Katie Kissinger's book, *All the Colors We Are: The Story of How We Get Our Skin Color*. (Each page features both Spanish and English.)
✓ Talking about the colors' associations constitutes *language arts*.
✓ Counting the number of different responses for each color includes *mathematics*.
✓ Incorporate *music* by inviting the children to march to Hap Palmer's "Parade of Colors" from his *Can a Cherry Pie Wave Goodbye?*

What Else I Did

_____

_____

_____

_____

_____

_____

_____

_____

Primary Colors

What It Teaches
- ✓ Color discrimination
- ✓ Primary colors
- ✓ Self-expression
- ✓ Cooperation

What You'll Need
- ✓ Objects or paint samples in red, yellow, and blue
- ✓ Red, yellow, and blue paint (optional)

What to Do
- ✓ Show the children red, yellow, and blue paint samples – or objects – explaining that these are the three primary colors from which other colors are created.
- ✓ Divide the class into three groups, assigning each a primary color.
- ✓ Challenge the members of each group to think of and demonstrate as many different things in their color as they can.

How to Ensure Success

Demonstrating with paints, sheer scarves, color palettes, or cellophane can help the children see how the three primary colors create others. Show them, or let them discover for themselves, what happens when red and yellow, red and blue, and yellow and blue are mixed.

Allow the children to demonstrate their responses individually, with others in the group, or with the group as a whole – whatever they find most appropriate. For example, if yellow reminds one child of the sun, she might want to act as the center, with the rest of her group surrounding her as the rays, or another child might choose to simply "shine" on his own.

What Else You Can Do
- ✓ Once the children understand this concept, you can begin "mixing" them: Assign one child from each group to partner with a child from a different group. Each pair then depicts something in the color they've created with their joining (you can tell them what color it is, if necessary). For instance, if a child from the red group and a child from the blue group form a pair, they must create something purple. You can ask all the pairs to work concurrently, or you can ask one pair at a time for a response, which they demonstrate for the rest of the class and the class guesses what the response is.

More Curriculum Connectors

✓ The self-expression and cooperation required in these activities fall under the heading of *social studies*.
✓ You and the children can count the number of different responses for each color to incorporate *mathematics*.
✓ You might include *language arts* by introducing (or reintroducing) the children to Tana Hoban's book *Is It Red? Is It Yellow? Is It Blue?* or Eric Carle's *My Very First Book of Colors*.
✓ Include Hap Palmer's "Colors" (from Volume I of *Learning Basic Skills Through Music*) and "Parade of Colors" (from Volume II) to incorporate *music*.

What Else I Did

_____
_____
_____
_____
_____
_____
_____
_____

Unit 5
Texture

Soft and Hard

What It Teaches
- ✓ Texture awareness
- ✓ Experience with the sense of touch
- ✓ The movement element of **force**[6]

What You'll Need
- ✓ A variety of both soft and hard objects (possibilities for soft items include stuffed animals, facial tissue, blankets, swatches of velvet or flannel; hard items might include a rock, key, coin, or marble)
- ✓ Loud and soft music (optional)
- ✓ A statue and a rag doll (optional)

What to Do
- ✓ Allow the children to touch all the objects.
- ✓ Ask them to tell you what they think the differences are between hard and soft.
- ✓ Now ask them to demonstrate the difference by making their bodies and/or body parts hard and soft.

How to Ensure Success

The children may find it easier at first to perform locomotor (traveling) movements that demonstrate the difference between hard and soft – for example, stamping for hard and tiptoeing for soft. Later, you can ask them to show you, with their muscles alone, remaining in one spot (tightening the muscles for hard and relaxing them for soft).

Using loud and soft music might help make these concepts less abstract. Loud music tends to inspire forceful (hard) movements, and soft music, gentle (soft) movements.

What Else You Can Do
- ✓ Introduce the children to a variety of soft and hard textures outdoors – for example, a flower's petals and a rock.
- ✓ Ask the children to think about the difference in texture between a statue and a ragdoll (show them both, if possible). Which is harder, and which is softer? Ask them to show you what they'd look like if they were statues, then ragdolls. Once they can demonstrate the difference in muscle tension, alternately call out the words *statue* and *ragdoll*, challenging the children to match the word called with the appropriate body posture. Vary the amount of time between words. (Because this is technically contracting and releasing muscles, you can use this as a relaxation exercise. Just be sure to end with the

---

[6] **force** The element of movement referring to its strength or weight and the amount of muscle tension applied.

ragdoll!)

More Curriculum Connectors

✓ Exploring the concepts of touch and muscle tension are both *science* activities. You also might explore the scientific concept of *cause and effect* by letting an ice cube or a stick of butter sit out all day. What happens? The children then can demonstrate melting with their bodies.

✓ Using soft and loud *music* will add yet another content area.

✓ Discussing the differences between textures is a *language arts* experience.

What Else I Did

_____
_____
_____
_____
_____
_____
_____
_____
_____

Smooth and Rough

What It Teaches
- ✓ Texture awareness
- ✓ Experience with the sense of touch
- ✓ The movement element of **flow**[7]

What You'll Need
- ✓ A variety of both smooth and rough objects (possibilities for smooth items include a marble, mirror, and swatch of satin or plastic; rough objects could include burlap, rope, and sandpaper)

What to Do
- ✓ Allow the children to touch all the objects.
- ✓ Ask the children to tell you what they think the differences are between smooth and rough.
- ✓ Ask them to show you the difference between moving smoothly and moving roughly.

How to Ensure Success
Providing familiar images might help the children understand these concepts better. For example, ice skaters gliding and eagles soaring move smoothly, while wind-up toys and robots move roughly.

What Else You Can Do
- ✓ Explore the possibilities for smooth and rough textures outdoors – for example, the bark of a tree and a pine needle.
- ✓ Increase comprehension of certain descriptive words by calling out a variety of them relative to *smooth* and *rough* and challenging the children to demonstrate their meanings. Possibilities to inspire smooth movement include *lightly, gliding, flowing,* and *floating*. Words that can conjure up rough movement include *jerky, stop-and-go, bumpy,* and *jagged*.
- ✓ Once the children understand the meanings of these words, alternate calling out a "smooth" word with a "rough" one, challenging them to change their movements accordingly.

More Curriculum Connectors
- ✓ Exploring the sense of touch involves *science*.
- ✓ Discussing the differences between smooth and rough and exploring descriptive words fall under the heading of *language arts*. You also might introduce the children to Dana

---

[7] **flow** The element of movement referring to its continuity (free flow) or lack thereof (bound flow).

Meachen Rau's book, *Soft and Smooth, Rough and Bumpy: A Book About Touch.*

What Else I Did

_____

_____

_____

_____

_____

_____

_____

_____

_____

Feathers and Seashells and Bears, Oh My

What It Teaches
- ✓ Awareness of texture
- ✓ Experience with the sense of touch
- ✓ Self-expression

What You'll Need
- ✓ Items of various textures (for example: rope, burlap, feathers, beach ball, stuffed animal, carpet square, facial tissue)

What to Do
- ✓ Talk to the children about how each item feels or makes them feel (a feather, for instance, might make them feel ticklish, while burlap makes them itchy).
- ✓ Ask the children to demonstrate their responses through movement.

How to Ensure Success
If the children need prompting, be more direct with your questions. For example: How would your body move if you were feeling ticklish? Itchy all over?

What Else You Can Do
- ✓ An alternative activity is to ask the children to move *like* the item exhibited. For example: how does a feather move? A teddy bear? A beach ball?
- ✓ Challenge the children to move all around the room, feeling for different textures. Can they create different sounds and rhythms with these textures? (For instance, a carpet makes a different sound than a chalkboard.) Can they move to the sounds and rhythms they create?

More Curriculum Connectors
- ✓ The sense of touch also relates to *science*.
- ✓ Self-expression is one of the early stages of *social studies*.
- ✓ *Music* is about creating sounds.
- ✓ Discussing how the various items feel relates to *language arts*. You also might incorporate Tana Hoban's book *Is It Rough? Is It Smooth? Is It Shiny?* into the exploration of this topic.

What Else I Did

_____

_____

_____

Section Two

LANGUAGE ARTS

The language arts include the interrelated and overlapping components of listening, speaking, reading, and writing. Therefore, because it is about communication – imparted or received – this content area plays a vital role in everyone's life. It also is part of every curriculum, in one form or another, from preschool through advanced education. Also, literacy is granted enormous validation in our society.

In early childhood programs, language arts traditionally have received the greatest concentration during daily group or circle times. During these periods, teachers and caregivers read stories or poems to the children, who sit and listen. Sometimes discussion precedes or follows the readings. In elementary schools, reading and writing have been handled all too commonly as separate studies, with the children focusing on topics such as phonics, spelling, and grammar.

A developmentally appropriate approach to children's emerging literacy recognizes that listening, speaking, reading, and writing overlap and interrelate, each contributing to the growth of the others. This approach also acknowledges that children learn best those concepts that are relevant to them. Therefore, their language acquisition and development must be a natural process that occurs over time, relates to all aspects of the children's lives, and *actively* involves the children in making meaning.

Movement, like language, plays an essential role in life and is also a form of communication. Body language is a distinct form of communication. Thus, movement and the language arts are naturally linked. Teachers who adopt an integrated approach to literacy soon realize that movement is a vital tool in the acquisition and development of the language arts. They also realize that there's no end to the number of ways to explore the language arts through movement!

Unit 6
Listening

What It Teaches
✓ **Auditory discrimination**[8]
✓ Memory

What You'll Need
No equipment or materials needed

What to Do
✓ Sitting on the floor with the children, tell them you're going to give them three different words, all beginning with the letter s, and that each has a different action.
✓ When they hear you say the word *seal*, have them clap their hands in front of them. When you say the word *sunshine*, ask them to make a circle with their arms above their heads. When they hear you say the word *salute*, have them perform a salute with hand to the forehead.
✓ Play the game for as long as the children stay interested, constantly mixing up the order of the words.

How to Ensure Success
Explain that they must listen very carefully, beyond the initial sound of the word, before performing the action. You're not trying to trick them; you want to see how well they can listen!

What Else You Can Do
✓ To make the game even more challenging, add some other words beginning with s, for which the children are not expected to perform an action. (Possibilities include *sandwich, snowshoe, sink, smile,* and *submarine.*) The extra words mean they'll really have to listen carefully.
✓ Play the game with words beginning with other letters.

More Curriculum Connectors
✓ Sound discrimination is also part of *music*. Ella Jenkins' album, *And One and Two*, was especially designed to help preschool and pre-primary children develop their listening skills.
✓ Focusing on the sense of hearing falls under the heading of *science*.

---

[8] **auditory discrimination** The ability to distinguish among sounds heard.

What Else I Did

_____

_____

_____

_____

_____

_____

_____

_____

Get into Action

What It Teaches
- ✓ **Auditory sequential memory**[9]
- ✓ Listening skills

What You'll Need
No equipment or materials needed

What to Do
- ✓ Tell the children you're going to give them a list of movements to do but that they're not to start doing them until you've finished speaking.
- ✓ Start with a short sequence – for example, *clap twice, blink eyes*.
- ✓ As the children are ready, lengthen the sequence – for example, *clap twice, blink eyes, turn around (jump in place, sit down*, etc.).

How to Ensure Success
Begin by performing the actions with the children as you say the words. When the children are ready, eliminate your actions.

What Else You Can Do
- ✓ Eliminate lines from familiar fingerplays (while still performing the actions) to test the children's memories and listening skills.

More Curriculum Connectors
- ✓ Because listening is related to the sense of hearing, these activities also are related to *science*.
- ✓ Sequencing is also part of *mathematics*.
- ✓ Musical fingerplays such as "Where Is Thumbkin?" and "The Eensy Weensy Spider" will connect the extended activity to *music*.

What Else I Did

_____

_____

_____

_____

_____

_____

---

[9] **auditory sequential memory** The ability to remember sounds or words in sequence.

How Many Sounds?

What It Teaches
- ✓ Auditory discrimination
- ✓ Listening skills
- ✓ Problem solving

What You'll Need
- ✓ A sheet of 8½" X 11" paper

What to Do
- ✓ Tell the children you're going to pass around a sheet of paper and you want each of them to create a different sound with it. (Possibilities include crumpling, tearing, flicking it with a finger, folding and unfolding, etc.)

How to Ensure Success
If the children get stumped, challenge them to use body parts other than the hands to create sounds. (Possibilities include rubbing the paper on the head, crumpling it underfoot, tapping it with a toe, blowing across it, or bouncing it off a knee.)

What Else You Can Do
- ✓ Go on a "listening walk," asking the children to identify all the sounds they hear (for example, footsteps, automobiles, birds). When you get back to class, challenge them to depict the actions of some of the creatures and objects they heard.
- ✓ You can also use the recorder on your smartphone as you go on the listening walk. When you return to the classroom, ask the children to first identify and then depict the sources of the sounds on the recording.

More Curriculum Connectors
- ✓ Listening is related to the sense of hearing, which is related to *science*.
- ✓ The creation of sounds is what *music* is all about.

What Else I Did

_____
_____
_____
_____
_____
_____

What's That Sound?

What It Teaches
- ✓ Auditory discrimination
- ✓ Listening skills

What You'll Need
- ✓ A variety of objects with familiar sounds (such as keys rattling or a door closing)
- ✓ Recording of familiar sounds (optional)

What to Do
- ✓ Ask the children to close their eyes; you then make a sound with one of the objects.
- ✓ Ask the children to identify the sound.
- ✓ Challenge them to show you, through movement or body shape, the item creating the sound.

How to Ensure Success
Encourage the children to respond either by taking on the shape of the object identified or by performing its movement.

What Else You Can Do
- ✓ As an alternative, make a recording of familiar sounds (for example, an electric can opener, a clock ticking, a door closing, or a vacuum cleaner) and play it for the children. This allows the activity to include a broader range of sounds.
- ✓ Record the children's voices at various times. Then play the recording and have the children try to identify which of their friends is talking!

More Curriculum Connectors
- ✓ Listening is related to the sense of hearing, which also makes it part of *science*.
- ✓ Focused listening and auditory discrimination are essential to the understanding and enjoyment of *music*.

What Else I Did

_____
_____
_____
_____
_____
_____
_____

Unit 7
Speaking

What's in a Name?

What It Teaches
- ✓ The rhythm of words
- ✓ An introduction to syllables

What You'll Need
No equipment or materials needed

What to Do
- ✓ Sit in a circle with the children and explain that they're going to discover the rhythm of their names.
- ✓ Go around the circle, clapping one child's name at a time – one clap per syllable – as you say the name aloud. *Billy Jones*, for example, would be Bil-ly Jones: three claps with a pause between the second and third.
- ✓ After you've spoken and clapped the rhythm of a name, have the children as a group echo you.

How to Ensure Success
Say and clap the names as slowly as necessary.

Depending on the age and developmental levels of the children, do both first and last names or first names only.

If the children are having trouble echoing you, repeat the name until most can respond successfully.

Be sure the children are saying the names aloud as they clap them.

What Else You Can Do
- ✓ Once the children can clap the syllables of their names, add foot stamping – one stamp per syllable. Start with the children still seated and eventually graduate to stepping in place and, finally, to one step per syllable, moving around the room.
- ✓ Once the children have mastered names, clap out the syllables of lines from nursery rhymes, poems, or favorite stories. For example: *Ma-ry had a lit-tle lamb.* Begin slowly and eventually increase the tempo.

More Curriculum Connectors
- ✓ Rhythm is a part of *music*.
- ✓ Point out the number of syllables in each child's name, perhaps even grouping the

children by syllables (or letting them group themselves), to include *mathematics*.

What Else I Did

_____
_____
_____
_____
_____
_____
_____
_____
_____

What It Teaches
- ✓ Connects cognitive, affective, and physical domains
- ✓ Self-expression
- ✓ Relevance to events in children's lives

What You'll Need
No equipment or materials needed

What to Do
- ✓ Choose a category you'd like to discuss with the children. For instance, ask them to tell you about their favorite birthday present, what they enjoyed most about their weekend, their favorite animals, etc.
- ✓ Ask one child to verbally relate his or her response to your question. Then ask the child to demonstrate through movement.
- ✓ Ask all the other children to imitate the movement.
- ✓ Repeat, giving each child a turn to initiate the discussion and movement.

How to Ensure Success
Encourage the children to either take on the shape of, for example, a favorite animal or perform its movements. Similarly, have them show you the shape of a favorite gift or depict its function. This allows the children to demonstrate both animate and inanimate favorites.

Because this is a relatively lengthy activity, you might choose to do it over several days rather than in one sitting, to prevent restlessness.

What Else You Can Do
- ✓ Have the children act out fairy tales and nursery rhymes to increase their comprehension and recall of the order of events. It's fun. Nursery rhymes such as "Jack and Jill," "Humpty Dumpty," and "Jack Be Nimble" (which also provides practice with jumping) are great for dramatization. Children's books that lend themselves to dramatization include *Caps for Sale* by Esphyr Slobodkina, *The Napping House* by Audrey Wood, and *Stellaluna* by Janell Cannon to name a few. Ask the children to tell you about their favorite parts or their favorite characters, and then depict their responses in movement.

More Curriculum Connectors
- ✓ The concept of shapes is related to *art*.
- ✓ Talking about holidays, families, and the like is part of *social studies*, and discussing

animals is relevant to *science*.

What Else I Did

_____
_____
_____
_____
_____
_____
_____
_____

Four Voices

What It Teaches
- ✓ Introduction to the "four voices" (the four different ways to use the human voice)
- ✓ Self-expression

What You'll Need
No equipment or materials needed

What to Do
- ✓ Explain the four different ways to use the human voice: whispering, speaking, shouting, and singing.
- ✓ Ask the children to tell you which of these is loudest and which is softest. If they were to think of whispering and shouting in terms of size, which would be biggest? What's the difference between speaking and singing? If they were to think of speaking and singing in terms of lines, which would be straight and which would be curvy?
- ✓ Ask the children to speak their names (you can do this one child at a time or have everyone do it at once). Repeat with the other three voices.
- ✓ Assign a specific kind of movement – perhaps with the children's collaboration – to each of the four voices. For example, whispering might be tiptoeing, speaking could be represented by a simple walk, shouting by stomping, and singing by dancing.
- ✓ Call out the kinds of voices, one at a time, and challenge each child to say her or his name while performing the corresponding movement.

How to Ensure Success
If this activity is too much for your group to handle all at once, concentrate on only one type of voice per day.

Demonstrate the four voices with your own name if you think it would be helpful.

Ask the children to echo what you do so they understand.

Be as direct in your instruction as you must be, based on the children's developmental levels. If they need to be reminded of the movement corresponding to the voice, that's what you should do.

What Else You Can Do
- ✓ Ask the children, one at a time, to demonstrate a movement representing one of the four voices – but without any accompanying sound. Ask the rest of the children to guess which voice it is.
- ✓ Recite nursery rhymes in each of the four voices.

More Curriculum Connectors

✓ The concept of four voices relates to *music*.

✓ Biggest and smallest are *mathematical* concepts, as are straight and curvy lines, which are also relevant to *art*.

✓ Self-expression falls under the heading of *social studies*.

What Else I Did

_____
_____
_____
_____
_____
_____
_____
_____
_____

Unit 8
Reading

Action!

What It Teaches
- ✓ Word comprehension
- ✓ Self-expression

What You'll Need
- ✓ A list of action words (possibilities include traveling words such as pounce, stamp, waddle, sneak, bounce, float, and slither; nontraveling action words include melt, collapse, shrink, shake, wriggle, and spin)
- ✓ A story with one or more action words in it (optional)

What to Do
- ✓ Post your list of action words, discussing what the children think each of them means.
- ✓ As you call out a word, have the children perform the corresponding action.

How to Ensure Success
Of course, you'll want to start with words the children know well or can readily understand. When necessary, demonstrate.

At first, alternate only a few words at a time. Add more as the children are ready.

Include some stopping action words as well. Possibilities include *freeze, pause, stop,* and *flop.*

What Else You Can Do
- ✓ Choose a story with one or more action words. After reading it aloud, choose a section including the word(s), and ask the children to act it out. Children's stories such as *The Little Engine That Could* and *Rosie's Walk* are among those that lend themselves to movement.
- ✓ When the children are ready, increase the challenge by presenting two words at a time. The children than create their own combinations, performing as many repetitions of each as desired, in any order.
- ✓ Do "The Freeze" from Greg and Steve's *We All Live Together, Volume 2.*

More Curriculum Connectors
- ✓ Self-expression falls under the heading of *social studies.*
- ✓ Greg and Steve's song brings in *music.*

What Else I Did

_____
_____
_____
_____
_____
_____
_____
_____

Descriptive Words

What It Teaches
✓ Word comprehension
✓ Self-expression

What You'll Need
✓ A list of descriptive words (possibilities include words such as graceful, light, forceful, smooth, droopy, gentle, strong, floppy, careful, enormous, tiny, excited)

What to Do
✓ Post your list, discussing what the children think each of the words means.
✓ As you call out a word, invite the children to perform a corresponding action.

How to Ensure Success
Start with words the children know well or can readily understand. Ask the children to tell you about the times they might have felt some of these things. If necessary, demonstrate.

At first, alternate only a few words at a time. Add more as the children are ready.

What Else You Can Do
✓ Ask the children to depict a person, character, animal, or object matching one of your descriptive words. For example, a giant is enormous, and a sad person might be droopy.
✓ Discover and act out some descriptive words inspired by the outdoors – for example, *breezy, sunny, warm, cool, muggy*.
✓ Children like to make up nonsense words. Ask each child to make up one word and, after saying it, demonstrate what it means.
✓ Read *The Teeny-Tiny Woman* by Paul Daldoni, and invite the children to act it out.

More Curriculum Connectors
✓ Self-expression is an important early part of *social studies*.
✓ To include *art*, ask the children to draw something that fits on of the descriptive words. You could also introduce the children to Tana Hoban's book of photographs, *Is It Rough? Is It Smooth? Is It Shiny?*

What Else I Did

_____
_____
_____

Happy Endings

What It Teaches
- ✓ Word comprehension
- ✓ An introduction to suffixes
- ✓ Self-expression

What You'll Need
No equipment or materials needed

What to Do
- ✓ Talk to the children about the difference between words such as *frightened* and *frightening*, *scared* and *scary*, *squeezed* and *squeezing*, *collapsed* and *collapsing*.
- ✓ Present the children with one word at a time, and challenge them to demonstrate the appropriate action or posture. Follow that with the same word with a different suffix. Are the children able to show you the difference in meaning?

How to Ensure Success
At this point, the children don't need to hear the word *suffixes*. Use the word *endings* instead, to avoid confusing them.

As you present each word, provide as much description or imagery as necessary to enhance comprehension. For example, you might be *scared* if you were watching a monster movie, but you'd be *scary* if you were the monster!

What Else You Can Do
- ✓ Make up a brief story that includes one word with different suffixes, and direct the children to act it out as you tell it.

More Curriculum Connectors
- ✓ Self-expression is related to *social studies*.

What Else I Did

_____

_____

_____

_____

_____

_____

_____

_____

Unit 9
Writing

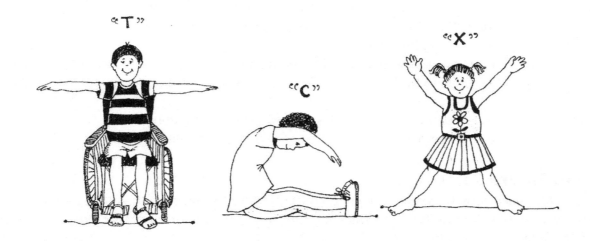

"T"

"C"

"X"

What It Teaches
- ✓ Preparation for writing (and reading)
- ✓ **Spatial awareness**[10]
- ✓ **Laterality**[11]
- ✓ Crossing the midline

What You'll Need
No equipment or materials needed

What to Do
- ✓ Have all the children sit or stand, facing the same direction.
- ✓ Use objects or places in the room to indicate which is their left side and which is their right side. For example, they may be sitting with the windows to their left and the door to their right.
- ✓ Invite them to perform the following activities – and others like them – always moving from left to right (for example, from the windows toward the door):
    - ➢ Turning the head
    - ➢ Drawing a line on the floor with a foot
    - ➢ Moving both arms at various levels in space (shoulder height, above the head, etc.)
    - ➢ Stepping (have them take several steps in sequence)
    - ➢ Jumping, hopping, or sliding (depending on skill levels)

How to Ensure Success
Before each activity, remind the children that they're to executive the movement from, for example, the side the windows are on to the side the door is on. Using the words *left to right* in conjunction with these physical reminders will help make the concept less abstract for them.

If necessary, demonstrate the movements until the children can be successful on their own. Be sure to sit or stand with your back to them so you're facing the same direction or, if you face them, remember to move from your right to left.

---

[10] **spatial awareness** Awareness of both personal and general space, involving levels (low, middle, and high), directions, and pathways (straight, curving, and zigzag).

[11] **laterality** A term that relates to the left and right sides of the body.

What Else You Can Do

✓ When they're ready, challenge the children to perform group activities that involve left-to-right movement(s). For example, they could hold hands and circle to the right, hold hands in a line and slide left to right, or do the "wave" from left to right.

✓ Perform the activities called for in Hap Palmer's "Left and Right," from *Getting to Know Myself.*

More Curriculum Connectors

✓ The spatial awareness involved is part of *art.*

✓ Any group activity involves cooperation, which is a component of *social studies.*

✓ Using the Hap Palmer song brings in *music.*

What Else I Did

_____

_____

_____

_____

_____

_____

_____

_____

What It Teaches
- ✓ Letter recognition
- ✓ Ability to physical replicate what the eyes see

What You'll Need
- ✓ Letters of the alphabet, for display
- ✓ Jump ropes (optional)
- ✓ Large, cut-out letters (optional)

What to Do
- ✓ Talk with the children about the straight, curving, and angled lines comprising the various letters of the alphabet.
- ✓ Choose a letter, point it out to the children, and ask them to make the letter with their body or body parts. Repeat with several letters.

How to Ensure Success

Begin with letters that are easiest to replicate. The fewer lines the letter has, the easier it is to reproduce. Some of the easiest are I, T, C, L, O, V, and X.

Allow the children to create either uppercase or lowercase letters.

What Else You Can Do
- ✓ Use jump ropes to create large letters on the floor. Challenge the children to follow, using various locomotor skills, the paths created by each letter. For example, you might invite them to first walk along the shape of each letter. Later, you could ask them to jump or gallop along it.
- ✓ When the children are ready to cooperate with others, have them form letters in pairs and, finally, trios. (Letters with three lines, such as H, are fun to do in trios.)
- ✓ For children who are developmentally ready, ask them to work in small groups to create short words, such as *hi* or *cat*.
- ✓ Scatter large letters on the floor throughout the room. Tell the children you're going to give them a locomotor skill to perform. On your signal, they move to any letter on the floor by executing the designated motor skill. Once at the letter, they take on its shape. Assign a new locomotor skill. At your next signal, the children move to new letters. The game continues until the children have moved, in as many different ways, to as many letters as possible. (Eventually, you can add adjectives to the game. For example, you might instruct the children to jog *slowly* to the next letter.)

More Curriculum Connectors

✓ Exploring shape is part of *art*.
✓ Straight, curving, and angled lines are explored in basic geometry, which falls under the heading of *mathematics*.
✓ Cooperating with others is part of *social studies*.
✓ To include music, choose "Marching Around the Alphabet" from Hap Palmer's *Learning Basic Skills Through Music*, Volume I.

What Else I Did

_____
_____
_____
_____
_____
_____
_____
_____
_____

Skywriting

What It Teaches
✓ Preparation for writing
✓ Spatial awareness

What You'll Need
The alphabet, posted where the children can easily see it

Recordings of several styles of music (optional)

What to Do
✓ Ask the children to imagine the air in front of them is a giant board and they've got a big marker – in any color they like – in their hands.
✓ Ask them to choose a letter from the alphabet and to "write" it on the "board."
✓ Continue with other letters. Can they write short words, or perhaps their names?

How to Ensure Success
Encourage the children to make their letters as large as possible at first, and gradually write them smaller and smaller.

Allow the children to make either uppercase or lowercase letters.

What Else You Can Do
✓ Encourage the children to use other body parts to "write" in the air. (Possibilities include elbows, top of the head, nose, and knees. The belly button is a favorite!)
✓ Ask the children to imagine that the floor in front of them is the board and they have a marker at the end of their toes. Can they make the letters with a foot?
✓ Have one child at a time write a letter. Ask the rest of the class to guess the letter.

More Curriculum Connectors
✓ The spatial awareness involved in these activities falls under the heading of *art*.
✓ Playing various styles of *music* in the background during these activities will add another content area to the mix, and also will change the way the children create their letters. For example, many classical pieces inspire long, smooth strokes, while rock and roll tends to inspire short, jabbing lines.

What Else I Did

_____

_____

Section Three

MATHEMATICS

To many adults, math is the most abstract of the content areas. We may have an aversion to this content area because we have failed in the past to do well in subjects such as algebra and calculus or on standardized tests (IQ or SATs). We may think balancing a checkbook or staying within budget is a complicated or unpleasant process.

But young children don't view math the same way we do; for them it isn't abstract. As Essa explains in *Introduction to Early Childhood Education* (Wadsworth Publishing, 2013), "The foundations of math are grounded in concrete experience such as the exploration of objects and gradual understanding of their properties and relationships. The cognitive concepts...of classification, seriation (ordering), numbers, time, and space all contribute to the gradual acquisition of math concepts."

Thus, the children are acquiring mathematical knowledge when they sort, stack, and compare manipulatives; play with sand and water; set the table or measure in the housekeeping center; or learn nursery rhymes and stories such as "The Three Little Kittens" and "Goldilocks and the Three Bears."

Quantitative ideas are also part of the language of mathematics. Mayesky, in *Creative Activities for Young Children* (Cengage Learning, 2014) recommends that the following words be incorporated into the children's daily routine:

big and little	few	bunch
long and short	tall and short	group
high and low	light and heavy	pair
wide and narrow	together	many
late and early	same length	more
first and last	highest	twice
middle	lowest	
once	longer than	

Obviously, physical activity can help children attach meaning to these words, as well as to numerals and other mathematical concepts so mathematics can continue to be a concrete rather than an abstract subject.

The mathematical concepts appropriate for exploration with young children include quantitative ideas, number awareness and recognition, counting, basic geometry, and simple addition and subtraction.

Unit 10

Quantitative & Positional Concepts

The Long and Short of It

What It Teaches
- ✓ **Quantitative concepts**[12]
- ✓ Comparison
- ✓ Opposites

What You'll Need
Straws or strips of paper in varying lengths and widths (optional)

What to Do
- ✓ Ask the children to demonstrate the following with their bodies: big, small, high, low, long, short, tall, wide, and narrow.
- ✓ Have them pair up, with partners demonstrating each of the following opposites: big/small, high/low, long/short, tall/short, and wide/narrow.
- ✓ With them still working in pairs, ask the children to demonstrate concepts such as: same length, longer than, shorter than, taller than, higher than, and wider than.

How to Ensure Success
It may be helpful to use visual aids for these activities. For example, you could use straws in varying lengths to display long, short, longer than, and shorter than. You could use strips of paper to demonstrate wide versus narrow.

You may want to spread these activities over several sessions.

What Else You Can Do
- ✓ After the children have experienced success with the preceding activities, challenge them to discover opposites for themselves. For example, ask them to demonstrate a wide shape. Once they have done so, ask them to show you the opposite of wide – without telling them what that is.
- ✓ With the children working in pairs, have one partner choose a shape to demonstrate, and the other depict its opposite.

More Curriculum Connectors
- ✓ These concepts also fall under the content area of *art*.
- ✓ Opposites are a component of *language arts*. You also can incorporate Tana Hoban's book, *Opposites*, into your lesson plan.

---

[12] **quantitative concepts** Mathematical ideas related to size, quantity, or relationships.

- ✓ Comparisons are often necessary in understanding certain *science* concepts.
- ✓ Working in partners constitutes *social studies*.

What Else I Did

_____
_____
_____
_____
_____
_____
_____
_____

Light and Heavy

What It Teaches
- ✓ Quantitative concepts
- ✓ Contrasting extremes
- ✓ The movement element of force

What You'll Need
Lightweight scarf or feather (optional)

What to Do
- ✓ Ask the children to sit and tap their fingers lightly on the floor in front of them. Then, in contrast, have them pound their fists on the floor. Continue to alternate between the two.
- ✓ Challenge the children to move their arms as lightly as possible, as though their arms were butterfly wings. Ask them to pretend that their arms are the propellers on a helicopter. Repeat several times.
- ✓ Have the children stand and show you what they'd look like if they were statues made of metal. What would they look like if they were ragdolls? Can they feel the difference in their muscles? Alternate calling out "statues" and "ragdolls," varying the amount of time in between.
- ✓ Ask the children to move as lightly as they can around the room, perhaps imagining that they're walking on eggs and don't want to break them. Then ask them to move while making as much noise with their feet as they possibly can.

How to Ensure Success
Use whatever imagery you think will help the children relate best to the concepts of light and heavy. For example, you may want to contrast a stalking cat with a dinosaur or a huge elephant for the last activity.

Although most children will have no problem with heavy – or strong – movement, they may find that moving lightly requires more control. To help inspire light movement, use a lightweight scarf or a feather to demonstrate.

What Else You Can Do
- ✓ Use action words that inspire light or heavy movement. For light, the possibilities include *tiptoe, stalk, float, flutter,* and *glide*. For heavy, the possibilities include *stomp, stamp, pounce, crash,* and *pound*. Talk about the meanings of these words before asking the children to demonstrate them.
- ✓ Use a drum or tambourine to signal changes from one kind of action to another. For example, bang slowly and heavily on the drum to inspire stomping, and tap more quickly

on it to inspire tiptoeing. Or you could use recorded music that corresponds to some of the preceding words.

More Curriculum Connectors

✓ Exploring the extremes in the muscle tension required of light and strong movements qualifies as *science*.

✓ Action words fall under the heading of *language arts*. Read and have the children dramatize *Stomp, Stomp* by Bob Kolar, the story of a little dinosaur who likes to do things forcefully. Follow it with Diane Youngblood Donlon's *Tippee Tippee Tiptoe*.

✓ The final extension activity brings an element of *music* into the mix.

What Else I Did

_____

_____

_____

_____

_____

_____

_____

_____

What It Teaches
- ✓ Quantitative concepts
- ✓ Basic counting
- ✓ Problem solving
- ✓ Practice with **nonlocomotor skills**[13]

What You'll Need
One piece of paper and pencil per child (optional)

What to Do
- ✓ Choose any nonlocomotor skill (such as bending, shaking, swaying, or swinging) you want the children to practice. Ask them to execute the skill once. Challenge them to do it one more time. How many times have they performed the skill? Challenge them to do it twice more. Do they know how many they've performed now?
- ✓ Challenge them to find how many ways they can bend (or sit or turn), counting as they explore. Can they find one more?
- ✓ How many body parts can they shake (or stretch or swing)? Can they find one more?

How to Ensure Success
If the children have difficulty keeping track of their "discoveries," provide them each with a piece of paper and a pencil and direct them to make a slash mark for every possibility. Then help them tally their results.

What Else You Can Do
- ✓ Invite the children to discover which body part has the most possibilities for shaking (or bending or stretching or swinging). This requires a higher level of problem solving.

More Curriculum Connectors
- ✓ Comprehension of these quantitative terms is part of *language arts*.
- ✓ Exploration and discovery of this sort falls under the scope of *science*.

What Else I Did

_____

_____

_____

_____

[13] **nonlocomotor skills** Movements performed in place.

What It Teaches
- ✓ Positional concepts
- ✓ General space
- ✓ Practice with **locomotor skills**[14]
- ✓ Cooperation

What You'll Need
Carpet squares or poly spots (optional)

What to Do
- ✓ Have the children take partners, with one child standing in front of the other and both facing the same direction. The child in front is to lead his or her partner throughout the room, with the partner in back "shadowing" every move. After a while, the children reverse leads. (Be sure to use the words *in front of* and *behind* in your descriptions.)

How to Ensure Success
Before undertaking this activity, talk to the children about shadows.

To ensure variety of movements, challenge the leaders to try different locomotor skills, levels, pathways, and body shapes.

What Else You Can Do
- ✓ Once the children have had ample practice in pairs, have them try this activity in groups of three (one leader and two shadows). Be sure to use the words *in the middle* and *between* in your descriptions. After a while, the first in line becomes the last in line, and so forth.
- ✓ Give each child a carpet square or poly spot to place on the floor, making sure they each have enough personal space. Issue challenges for the children to stand in various ways in relation to the carpet square. Possibilities include *on it*, *behind it*, *in front of it*, *beside it*, and *over it*.
- ✓ On a bright and sunny day, bring the children outdoors to play with their *real* shadows. How many ways can they get their shadows to move?

More Curriculum Connectors
- ✓ The concept of shadows falls under the heading of *science*.
- ✓ Because the shadow game is a cooperative activity, it also is part of *social studies*.
- ✓ The prepositions explored in these activities are a part of speech and, therefore, of

---

[14] **locomotor skills** Traveling movements that transport the body as a whole from one point to another.

language arts.

✓ Exploring a variety of pathways, levels, and shapes is an *art* concept. You also might introduce the children to Tana Hoban's photos in *Shadows and Reflections*. To incorporate both *art* and *language arts*, choose Stephen R. Swinburne's *Guess Whose Shadow?*

What Else I Did

_____
_____
_____
_____
_____
_____
_____
_____
_____

Over the River and Through the Woods

What It Teaches
- ✓ Positional concepts
- ✓ Spatial awareness
- ✓ Problem solving

What You'll Need
Materials for an obstacle course (classroom furniture, cardboard boxes, jump ropes, hoops, etc.)

Display cards with written or drawn directions

What to Do
- ✓ Set up a simple obstacle course.
- ✓ At each point on the course, display a card with a written or drawn instruction (or both) indicating whether the children should move *over, under, around,* or *through* an obstacle.
- ✓ Once the children have traversed the course several times, change it slightly (for example, rearrange the order of the obstacles). Also, if the children were previously expected to go *over* a hoop lying flat, you might stand the hoop in a holder and redirect them to travel *through* the hoop.

How to Ensure Success
Move through the course once yourself – with or without the children – to ensure they fully understand what's expected of them.

If you have several children waiting their turn, to avoid the disruptions that often result from impatience, give the children in line an assignment. For instance, have them create shapes with their bodies and body parts that someone or something could possibly move *over, under, around,* or *through.* If there's enough room, divide the class in half and have the two groups move through the course simultaneously, beginning on opposite sides.

What Else You Can Do
- ✓ When the children are ready for more challenging problem solving, choose an item – such as a hula hoop or a balance beam – and ask them to find two or three different ways to move *over, along,* or *beside* it.
- ✓ Extend the activity further by inviting the children to move, for instance, one-half, three-quarters, or two-thirds of the way across a balance beam. (Marking the beam with labeled pieces of masking tape ensures success.)
- ✓ Create an obstacle course outside that includes some natural obstacles, such as trees to

move around or small rocks to leap over.

More Curriculum Connectors

✓ Because these positional concepts are prepositions, this activity also involves *language arts*.

✓ Spatial relationships are involved, too, which relate to *art*. You might want to share Tana Hoban's *Over, Under, and Through* with the children.

✓ To reinforce these positional concepts, sing and discuss songs such as "Over the River and Through the Woods," "Somewhere Over the Rainbow," "Ring Around the Rosie," "The Bear Went Over the Mountain," or "She'll Be Comin' 'Round the Mountain" (*music*).

What Else I Did

_____
_____
_____
_____
_____
_____
_____
_____

Unit 11
Number Awareness & Recognition

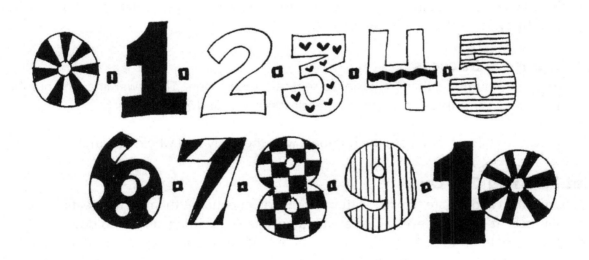

Number Shapes I

What It Teaches
- ✓ Number awareness and recognition
- ✓ Ability to physically replicate what the eyes see
- ✓ Experience with the movement element of shape

What You'll Need
Large numbers 0 through 9 for posting

Large cut-out numbers (optional)

What to Do
- ✓ Talk with the children about the straight, curving, and angled lines comprising the different numbers.
- ✓ Choose a number, point it out to the children, and ask them to make the number with their body. Repeat with several numbers.

How to Ensure Success
Begin with numbers that are easier to replicate than others. The fewer lines the number has, the easier is it to reproduce. The easiest are 0, 1, and 7.

Allow the children to create the numbers with the body as a whole or with body parts.

What Else You Can Do
- ✓ Once the children are familiar with this concept, encourage them to try creating the numbers at different levels, such as standing, kneeling, sitting, and lying down.
- ✓ Ask the children to demonstrate the number that represents their age or to choose a number between, for example, 0 and 4 or 5 and 9.
- ✓ When the children are ready to cooperate with others, have them form numbers in pairs and, finally, trios. (Numbers with three lines, such as 4, are fun to do in trios.)
- ✓ Place large cut-out numbers on the floor throughout the room. At your signal, have the children move in a predesignated way (such as galloping) to any number they want, taking on the shape of that number once they arrive. Change the way in which they're to move to another number, give the signal again, and continue the game.

More Curriculum Connectors
- ✓ Exploring shapes is part of *art*.
- ✓ Cooperating with others comes under the heading of *social studies*.
- ✓ Volume I of Hap Palmer's *Learning Basic Skills Through Music* includes "The Number

March" (*music*).

What Else I Did

_____
_____
_____
_____
_____
_____
_____
_____
_____

Number Shapes II

What It Teaches
- ✓ Number awareness and recognition
- ✓ Ability to physically replicate what the eyes see
- ✓ Shapes
- ✓ Practice with locomotor skills

What You'll Need
Large numbers 0 through 9 for posting

One jump rope per child

What to Do
- ✓ Provide each child with a jump rope, or something similar, with which to create the number you designate on the floor.
- ✓ Once the number is ready, challenge the children to trace its pathway with a locomotor skill that you select.

How to Ensure Success
Begin with numbers that have the simplest shapes.

Choose only locomotor skills the children can perform most easily.

If the children aren't developmentally ready to form the numbers themselves, create them yourself, perhaps even using masking tape.

What Else You Can Do
- ✓ Allow the children to choose their own numbers and even their own locomotor skills.
- ✓ As a more advanced activity, if your children are doing simple computation, challenge them to create the number they get when adding, for instance, 1 plus 1.

More Curriculum Connectors
- ✓ The exploration of shapes incorporates *art*.
- ✓ Physically replicating – "writing" the numbers on the floor – links this activity to *language arts*. You might also want to share Jean Marzollo's *I Spy Little Numbers* with the children.

What Else I Did

_____

_____

_____

_____

_____

_____

_____

_____

Invisible Numbers

What It Teaches
✓ Number awareness and recognition
✓ Preparation for writing
✓ Spatial awareness

What You'll Need
No equipment or materials needed

What to Do
✓ Ask the children to imagine that the air in front of them is a giant board and they've got a big piece of chalk – in any color they like – in their hands.
✓ Have them choose a number and "write" it on the "board."
✓ Continue with other numbers, asking the children to vary the numbers' sizes.

How to Ensure Success
Encourage the children to make their numbers as large as possible at first, gradually writing them smaller and smaller.

Begin with the simplest of numbers (those with the fewest lines, such as 0, 1, and 7) before moving on to numbers that are more difficult to draw (such as 5).

What Else You Can Do
✓ Ask the children to imagine the floor in front of them is the board and they have a marker/chalk at the end of their toes. Can they make the numbers with a foot?
✓ Once the children can accomplish this, encourage them to use other body parts to "write" – on the board in the air or on the floor. Possible body parts include elbows, top of the head, nose, and knees. Writing with the belly button and bottom are particularly hilarious for the kids!
✓ Have one child at a time write a number. Ask the rest of the class to guess the number.

More Curriculum Connectors
✓ The spatial awareness involved in these activities is an *art* concept.
✓ Preparation for writing is part of *language arts*.
✓ If you play various styles of *music* in the background during these activities, you'll add another content area to the mix and also will change the style with which the children create their letters. To make a true cognitive connection, talk with the children about the different qualities of the music and how those qualities made them feel like writing.

What Else I Did

_____

_____

_____

_____

_____

_____

_____

_____

Unit 12

Counting

Blast Off!

What It Teaches
- ✓ Counting backward
- ✓ Number awareness
- ✓ Spatial awareness

What You'll Need
No equipment or materials needed

What to Do
- ✓ Ask the children to squat low, pretending to be spaceships on their launching pads.
- ✓ With as much drama as you can muster, count backward from 10 to 1.
- ✓ When you say "Blast off," have the children "launch" themselves upward and pretend to fly around in outer space.
- ✓ Repeat several times.

How to Ensure Success
Prior to the activity, talk to the children about space shuttles, launching pads, and blasting off.

Let the children know when to expect to hear "Blast off!"

Emphasize that once the "spaceships" are in the air, the children must maintain their own "personal space" so the spaceships won't collide.

What Else You Can Do
- ✓ Call out every other number yourself, with the children supplying the missing numbers. Eventually, have them do all the counting themselves.
- ✓ Use the "blast off" part of this exercise every time you're moving from an activity that takes place sitting to one in which you want the children to stand. It's a lot more fun than simply telling them to stand up!

More Curriculum Connectors
- ✓ The concept of space travel is part of *science*.
- ✓ The spatial awareness involved, particularly the levels through which the children move, is a component of *art*.
- ✓ Any discussion of an astronaut as a choice of occupation would fall under the heading of *social studies*.
- ✓ Add a *language arts* component by reading Molly Bang's *Ten, Nine, Eight*.

What Else I Did

_____
_____
_____
_____
_____
_____
_____
_____

How Many Parts?

What It Teaches
- ✓ Counting
- ✓ Body awareness
- ✓ **Divergent problem solving**[15]
- ✓ Balance

What You'll Need
No equipment or materials needed

What to Do
- ✓ Challenge the children to place a specified number of body parts on the floor.
- ✓ Repeat several times, varying the number of body parts. Also, sometimes challenge them to use the same number but different body parts. For example, a challenge to touch the floor with three body parts could result in two feet and a hand, two hands and a foot, two knees and a hand, etc.

How to Ensure Success
Begin with higher numbers (but not too high – perhaps 5 being the highest) so the children won't have trouble with balance.

Be sure to point out the variety of responses you see so the children understand there are many "correct" possibilities.

Because children think differently than we do, they may not always count body parts as we do. For example, sometimes the bottom is counted as one part and sometimes as two! Sometimes, for young children, a foot counts as five parts. Be sure you understand *what* and *how* they're counting before you determine they have a problem with it.

Sometimes, rather than labeling the parts you see (for example, "I see Leanne is using two elbows and two knees"), count body parts as you move throughout the room. Of course, if you've asked them to place four body parts on the floor, you should be counting 1 to 4 repeatedly; the repetition is helpful to the children.

What Else You Can Do
- ✓ Ask the children to count the number of seconds they can hold very still in each position. Once they're more adept at balance, challenge them to see how many seconds they can *balance* in each position.

---

[15] **divergent problem solving** Finding more than one solution to a single challenge.

More Curriculum Connectors

- ✓ Identifying body parts and balance are *science* concepts, as is finding the center of gravity, which the children must do if they're going to remain upright!
- ✓ *Language arts* possibilities include Larent de Brunhoff's *Babar's Counting Book*, *The Doorbell Rang* by Pat Hutchins, and *Count!* by Denise Fleming.
- ✓ *Island Counting 1-2-3* by Frane Lessac adds a cultural component, linking it to *social studies*.
- ✓ "The Body Poem," a song from Rae Pica and Richard Gardzina's *Wiggle, Giggle, & Shake* CD, points out the number of such body parts as hands, eyes, eyelids, elbows, and more and adds *music* to the mix.

What Else I Did

_____

_____

_____

_____

_____

_____

_____

_____

Oh, the Possibilities

What It Teaches
- ✓ Counting
- ✓ Problem solving
- ✓ Body awareness

What You'll Need
No equipment or materials needed

What to Do
- ✓ Ask the children to discover three different ways they can move an arm.
- ✓ Give them ample time to explore, and then repeat with a different body part. Possible parts include a leg, the head, a hand, or an elbow.

How to Ensure Success
If the children need some extra help from you, suggest that they try moving the parts in different directions and at different levels.

If necessary, explore, discover, and count with them.

Use the arm and hand as the easiest parts to begin with. Moving just one legs requires balance, and the head and elbows require a certain amount of body-part isolation, which is challenging for young children.

What Else You Can Do
- ✓ Once the children are more skilled at this, increase the number of ways you ask them to move each body part. You also might present the greater challenge of asking them to find *how many ways* they can move each part.
- ✓ Invite the children to discover how many steps (jumps, hops, etc.) it takes to get from one end of the room (or outdoor space) to the other.
- ✓ Ask them if the number changes if they cross diagonally.

More Curriculum Connectors
- ✓ Exploration and discovery, as well as problem solving, are vital to the nature of *science*.
- ✓ The spatial awareness involved in the alternate activity is a component of *art*.
- ✓ To add *music* and *language arts*, use some of the songs from Ella Jenkins' *Counting Games and Rhythms for the Little Ones*.

What Else I Did

_____
_____
_____
_____
_____
_____
_____
_____

Unit 13

Basic Geometry

Line 'Em Up

What It Teaches
- ✓ Basic geometry involving lines
- ✓ Shape
- ✓ Body awareness
- ✓ Ability to physically replicate what the eyes see

What You'll Need
Drawings of vertical, horizontal, diagonal, crossed, curved, and crooked lines

Masking tape, to create the various lines on the floor (optional)

What to Do
- ✓ Post the drawings of lines where the children can see them.
- ✓ Discuss each of these lines with your group.
- ✓ Ask the children to replicate each with their body or with individual body parts.

How to Ensure Success
When discussing the various lines, use imagery and phrases the children can relate to. For instance, a vertical line might be said to be "standing up," while a horizontal line is "lying down." Use the corners of the room when describing a diagonal line, which goes from corner to corner.

Begin with the simplest lines – vertical and horizontal. The most challenging are going to be diagonal and crossed.

What Else You Can Do
- ✓ Place masking tape on the floor, replicating the various types of lines, and ask the children to move along them. Begin with basic locomotor skills such as creeping or walking, changing the skill every time the children complete one pass. As a more advanced challenge, assign a different locomotor skill for each type of line.
- ✓ Challenge the children to create the lines with partners.
- ✓ Ask the children to discover examples of the different lines throughout the room. Then present challenges such as, "Show me the kind of line the flagpole makes."

More Curriculum Connectors
- ✓ Shape and line are *art* concepts.
- ✓ Working in cooperation with a partner is a part of *social studies*.
- ✓ The ability to physically replicate what the eyes see is necessary in writing, which is part

of *language arts*. Marisabina Russo's *The Line Up Book* is a fun story about a little boy's need to create a line.

What Else I Did

_____
_____
_____
_____
_____
_____
_____
_____

On the Right Path

What It Teaches
✓ Recognition of lines
✓ Pathways
✓ Practice with locomotor skills

What You'll Need
Masking tape, rope, chalk, or something similar to create pathways on the floor (optional)

Carpet squares or hoops (optional)

What to Do
✓ Beginning with the locomotor skill of walking, ask the children to travel about the room. Challenge them to move only in straight paths at first.
✓ Once the children have succeeded in traveling in straight pathways, ask them to make curving and, finally, zigzagging pathways.
✓ Follow the same pattern with other locomotor skills (run, jump, leap, gallop, hop, slide, skip).

How to Ensure Success
Demonstrate straight, curving, and zigzag pathways for the children, perhaps initially playing a brief game of Follow the Leader.

If necessary, create the three types of pathways on the floor with masking tape, chalk, or rope.

What Else You Can Do
✓ Challenge the children to move along straight, curving, and zigzag pathways in backward and sideward directions.
✓ Play a game called Come to Me. In this game, the children scatter throughout the room, each finding her or his own personal space. (If the children will have trouble remembering their spots, provide them with carpet squares, poly spots, or hoops.) Then stand in the center of the room and instruct the children to come to you in various ways. For example, to gain additional practice with pathways, you might say, "Come to me, traveling in a straight path from your spot." After all the children have arrived at your spot, give them instructions for returning to their personal spaces (for example, "Return to your personal space, traveling in a curvy pathway"). Once the children are handling one instruction at a time, increase the challenge by combining two instructions (for instance, "Come to me at a low level, moving in a zigzagging pathway").

More Curriculum Connectors
- ✓ Line is an *art* concept.
- ✓ Include *language arts* by reading Paula Bossio's *The Line.*

What Else I Did

_____
_____
_____
_____
_____
_____
_____
_____
_____

Right to the Point

What It Teaches
- ✓ Recognition of points
- ✓ Shape
- ✓ Body awareness

What You'll Need
Miscellaneous items found throughout the classroom

What to Do
- ✓ Show the children examples of different points in the room (the point of a pencil, the corner of a chalkboard, the point of a clock hand, the corner of a book, etc.).
- ✓ Ask the children to first create a pointed shape with their fingers. Advance from there by challenging them to create pointed shapes with their arms and hands, their feet, and their body as a whole.

How to Ensure Success
Speak in terms of pointed *shapes*, instead of simply creating points, to make things clearer to the children.

If necessary, demonstrate several pointed shapes yourself.

What Else You Can Do
- ✓ Invite the children to create pointed shapes in pairs and trios.

More Curriculum Connectors
- ✓ The concept of points is also part of *art*.
- ✓ Working in pairs and trios is a part of *social studies*.

What Else I Did

_____
_____
_____
_____
_____
_____
_____
_____

What a Square!

What It Teaches
- ✓ Simple geometric shapes
- ✓ Body awareness

What You'll Need
Pictures of circles, triangles, and squares

Masking tape or rope (optional)

What to Do
- ✓ Post the pictures where the children can easily see them.
- ✓ Talk to the children about the straight and curving lines that make up each of these geometric shapes.
- ✓ Ask the children to replicate these three geometric shapes with their body or individual body parts.

How to Ensure Success
Point out that a circle is one continuous, curving line; a triangle is made up of three straight lines; and a square consists of four straight lines.

If necessary, first explore the possibilities for angles created by the body and body parts.

Encourage the children to create their shapes at various levels in space, such as lying, kneeling, and standing.

What Else You Can Do
- ✓ Have the children create their shapes in groups of two, three, and four.
- ✓ Create these shapes on the floor with masking tape or rope and ask the children to travel along the shapes using a variety of locomotor skills.
- ✓ Show the children a rectangle and challenge them to show you, with their body, the difference between a rectangle and a square.
- ✓ Challenge them to discover circles, triangles, squares, and rectangles throughout the room and outdoors. Ask them to show you, for example, the shape of the door, the top of the wastebasket, or a rooftop.

More Curriculum Connectors
- ✓ *Art* is also covered with these activities. Consider choosing from Tana Hoban's books *Circles, Triangles, and Squares*; *Round, Round, Round*; and *Shapes, Shapes, Shapes*.

✓ Working in pairs or groups is part of *social studies*.
✓ To include *language arts*, read Eric Carle's *My Very First Book of Shapes*.

What Else I Did

_____

_____

_____

_____

_____

_____

_____

_____

_____

Unit 14
Simple Computation

"Roll Over"

What It Teaches
- ✓ Subtraction
- ✓ Practice with **log rolls**[16]
- ✓ Cooperation

What You'll Need
Floor mat

Merle Peek's *Roll Over: A Counting Book* (optional)

What to Do
✓ If the children aren't familiar with the song "Roll Over," teach them the lyrics and discuss the song with them. The lyrics are as follows:

There were 10 in the bed,
And the little one said,
"Roll over, roll over."
So they all rolled over,
And one fell out.

There were 9 in the bed,
And the little one said...

One in the bed,
And the little one said,
"Alone at last!" (spoken)

✓ Choose 10 children to lie on the floor (or a floor mat, if possible), pretending they're lying in a bed. Then, as you and the remaining children sing the song, have the children on the floor act it out.
✓ Prior to each verse, ask the group to tell you how many children are remaining "in the bed."

How to Ensure Success
Before starting the song, have the children practice log rolls. Explain that they should keep their body as straight as a log and hide their ears with their arms as they roll over, beginning and ending on their back.

---

[16] **log rolls** Rolls in which the participant maintains a long, straight, body, usually with the arms overhead.

102

Practice "group rolling" with the children who are going to be "in the bed." Explain that they shouldn't roll until they hear the lyrics, "So they all rolled over."

You might want to start with a group of fewer than 10.

If members of your group will feel left out if they aren't included in the rolling, divide your class into groups of the same number and begin the song with that number. So, if you have 15 children in class, divide them into three groups of five each, then start the song with, "There were five in the bed."

What Else You Can Do
✓ Merle Peek has illustrated this song in the book *Roll Over: A Counting Book*. You could use the book instead of, or in addition to, singing the song.
✓ Act out the song, "The Three Little Monkeys." The lyrics are as follows:

Three little monkeys
Jumping on the bed,
One fell off and bumped his head,
Mother called the doctor and the doctor said,
"No more monkeys jumping on the bed."

Two little monkeys
Jumping on the bed,
One fell off and bumped his head,
Mother called the doctor and the doctor said,
"No more monkeys jumping on the bed."

One little monkey
Jumping on the bed,
One fell off and bumped his head,
Mother called the doctor and the doctor said,
"Get those monkeys back to bed."

More Curriculum Connectors
✓ The song places this activity under the heading of *music*.
✓ The cooperation involved in rolling over together is an aspect of *social studies*.
✓ The song lyrics are a part of *language arts* – which you'll be further addressing if you use Sandra Boynton's *Hippos Go Berserk*, which adds and subtracts hippopotami!

What Else I Did

_____

_____

_____

_____

_____

_____

_____

_____

Add 'Em & Subtract 'Em

What It Teaches
- ✓ Counting
- ✓ Simple addition and subtraction
- ✓ Levels in space

What You'll Need
Numbered cards (optional)

What to Do
- ✓ Have the children sit in a circle on the floor or on the ground.
- ✓ Call out a child's name. Have that child get up and stand in the center of the circle.
- ✓ Ask the children how many are in the center. When they've responded correctly, call out another child's name and ask him or her to join the child already in the center.
- ✓ Ask the children how many are in the circle now.
- ✓ Continue adding – and subtracting—children, each time asking the group to tell you how many are standing in the center.

How to Ensure Success
Begin by adding and subtracting only one child at a time. Later, when the children are ready, add or subtract two or three children at a time.

Be sure to use the words *add* and *subtract* in your game. For example, you might say, "We've added *one* person to the *one* already in the circle. How many are in the circle now?"

You might want to call out the children's names in the order in which they're sitting (perhaps nearest to farthest from you) so they don't get the feeling you're choosing favorites first. Another way is to close your eyes and point.

What Else You Can Do
- ✓ Vary the locomotor skills used to enter and leave the circle. Assign a skill, or let the children choose.
- ✓ Instead of playing this game in a circle, call the children by name – one, two, or three at a time – to the front of the room. When it's time to subtract children, simply ask them to return to their seats.
- ✓ If your children are ready for more challenging computation, give each of them a number written on a card. Call two children at a time to the center of the circle (or front of the room), and ask the remaining children to add (or subtract) the numbers on the cards.

More Curriculum Connectors

✓ Whichever version of the game you play, the children will be moving from low to high levels and back again. These positional concepts address another aspect of mathematics (quantitative concepts) and *art* as well.

✓ To add *music* to math lessons, consider Hap Palmer's *Math Readiness: Addition and Subtraction*.

✓ For *language arts*, Eric Carle's *The Very Hungry Caterpillar* is a wonderful counting book.

What Else I Did

_____
_____
_____
_____
_____
_____
_____
_____
_____

How Many Parts Now?

What It Teaches
- ✓ Counting
- ✓ Basic addition and subtraction
- ✓ Body awareness
- ✓ Balance
- ✓ Divergent problem solving

What You'll Need
Floor mats (optional)

What to Do
- ✓ This is a variation of "How Many Parts" (presented previously), in which you asked the children to place certain numbers of body parts on the floor. With this game, you'll start off the same way but then ask the children to add or subtract one (or two or three) part(s) to or from those already touching the floor. For instance, begin by asking the children to put three body parts on the floor. Once they've accomplished this, ask them to add or subtract one body part.
- ✓ After each challenge to add or subtract a part or parts, ask the children to tell you how many parts they now have touching the floor.

How to Ensure Success
Start by asking the children to place just two or three parts on the floor and to add or subtract from those.

At first, add or subtract only one body part at a time. When they're ready, move on to two and, finally, three parts.

Point out the different responses you see (for example, one child might have a hand and a foot touching the floor while another has chosen a knee and a hand) so the children understand that there are lots of "right" answers.

What Else You Can Do
- ✓ For more of a challenge, add and subtract numbers of body parts touching *each other*.
- ✓ For a cooperative activity, call for a certain number of children to connect – at the elbows, for example. Then add and subtract from there. (Try to divide the class evenly so no children are left out. For instance, if you have 15 in a class, group them by either threes or fives.)

More Curriculum Connectors

✓ Body awareness and balance are *science* concepts.
✓ Working cooperatively is part of *social studies*.
✓ *The Doorbell Rang* by Pat Hutchins, a *language arts* tool, is excellent for teaching simple computation.
✓ Addition and subtraction are among the concepts covered with *music* in Hap Palmer's *Math Readiness*.

What Else I Did

_____
_____
_____
_____
_____
_____
_____
_____

Section Four

MUSIC

It's impossible to think of music and movement as completely separate entities. Music educator Carl Orff based his approach on the belief that music, movement, and speech are interrelated. Jaques-Dalcroze believed that traditional methods of training musicians concentrated too heavily on the intellect, thereby neglecting the senses.

Not only did educators like Dalcroze and Orff consider music and movement inseparable, but children do too. For young children, experiencing music is simply not limited to the auditory sense, as evidenced by even infants' "whole-body" responses to music.

Unfortunately, too often a child's musical ability is judged by an ability to sing or play an instrument. Even if a child possesses such talent, if his exposure to music is limited to one of those two avenues, he isn't experiencing music to the fullest. And what of the child who shows no interest, or aptitude for, singing or playing an instrument?

If all children are to experience music fully, they should explore it as a whole, being given opportunities to listen, sing, play, create, and *move*. When a child tiptoes to soft music, stamps her feet to soft music, moves in slow motion to Bach's Air on the G String," then rapidly to Rimsky-Korsakov's "Flight of the Bumblebee," sways to a 3/4 meter, and skips to a piece in 6/8, she is experiencing the music on many levels. Beyond listening, she is using her body, mind, and spirit to express and create. Because she's using a multimodal approach, what she learns will make a lasting impression.

Some musical concepts are too advanced for young children to grasp. Others are important only to those who go on to study music seriously. But young children can and should experience many musical elements, including tempo, volume, staccato and legato, pitch, mood, and rhythm.

Tempo is the speed at which the music is performed, which means that this musical element is related to the movement element of time. The best way to introduce tempo is by contrasting the extremes – very slow and very fast. Once children can recognize and move to fast and slow music, you will begin to introduce the more challenging concept of the continuum from very slow to very fast, and the reverse. *Accelerando* is the term for music that begins slowly and increases gradually in tempo. *Ritardando* indicates a gradually decreasing tempo.

Volume refers specifically to the loudness or softness of sounds. Although many people incorrectly associate big or high movements with loud music, and small, low movements with soft music, this musical element truly goes hand in hand with the movement element of force. When the music is soft, moving with a great deal of muscle tension or strength would be an unlikely response. And when the music is loud, it isn't likely to conjure up, for example, images of butterflies floating.

Again, the best way to introduce volume is by contrasting extremes. Once the children can move well to loud and soft music, begin introducing the continuum from one to the other. *Crescendo* is the term for music that begins softly and gradually gets louder. *Decrescendo* refers to gradually decreasing volume.

Staccato and **legato** relate to the movement element of flow and are part of the broader category of articulation. On the one hand, *legato*, which corresponds to free flow (smooth, uninterrupted movement), indicates that the music is to be played without any noticeable interruptions between the notes, flowing smoothly. *Staccato*, on the other hand, is more punctuated and therefore corresponds with bound flow (interrupted or halting).

Pitch is the highness or lowness of a musical tone. With this concept, high and low movements are most appropriate.

Music often conveys feelings, and, very often, young children are the first to pick up on the **mood** of a song and respond to it. This ability seems related to the as-yet undiminished sensitivity of the young child's ear and to her or his as-yet undiminished willingness to show a physical response. Your role as a teacher is to make the children aware of how different music affects them. Talk to them about how certain songs make them feel, the musical elements involved, and why they think the songs evoke the responses they do.

Rhythm refers to the groupings of sounds, silences, and patterns. Within the context of this book, rhythm will consist of the concepts of **beat** and **meter**.

The *beat* in music is the recurring rhythmic pulse that is heard (and felt) throughout a piece. *Meter* indicates a basic group of beats. When a meter is stated, the top number refers to the number of beats in a measure; the bottom number indicates the *kind* of note that equals one beat. For example, 2/4 means that each measure has two *quarter*-notes, with 6/8 indicating six *eighth*-notes to the measure. A quarter-note can be likened to a walking step, as it takes approximately the same time to complete. An eighth-note is twice as fast as a quarter-note (more like a running step).

All of these musical elements can be explored through movement, offering the children a multisensory approach that gives the concepts greater meaning and promotes retention.

Unit 15
Tempo

Moving Slow/Moving Fast

What It Teaches
- ✓ Recognition and contrast of tempos
- ✓ Experience with the movement element of time
- ✓ Self-regulation
- ✓ Listening skills

What You'll Need
A hand drum and mallet or an alternative (a coffee can or an oatmeal container with a lid and a wooden spoon will do)

What to Do
- ✓ Talk to the children about very slow and very fast. What are times when they would move in either way?
- ✓ Ask the children to stand and move in the ways the drum makes them feel like moving. Then alternate between very slow and very fast beats.

How to Ensure Success
If the children have any trouble with this activity, offer suggestions of how they could move. For example, the slow beats might inspire giant steps, and the quick beats inspire tiny ones.

Be sure your beats demonstrate a vast difference between very slow and very fast. Contrasting extremes is the best way to introduce concepts such as slow and fast.

When you want the children to move slowly, *speak* slowly. When you want them to move quickly, pick up the pace of your speech.

What Else You Can Do
- ✓ The drum will inspire a great deal of excitement. Letting each child have a turn with it, dictating the group's movement, provides a real sense of power for them. (Don't worry if the children don't get the beating quite right at first.)
- ✓ Contrast slow and fast imagery. For example, invite the children to move like a turtle and then like a racehorse. Can they move like an inchworm and then like a bumblebee?

More Curriculum Connectors
- ✓ Listening skills are a part of *language arts*.
- ✓ Listening also is related to the sense of hearing, which falls under the heading of *science*.
- ✓ Self-regulation is part of the self-discovery that introduces *social studies*.

What Else I Did

_____
_____
_____
_____
_____
_____
_____
_____

Moving Slow/Moving Fast – Again

What It Teaches

- ✓ Recognition and contrast of tempos
- ✓ Experience with the movement element of time
- ✓ Self-regulation
- ✓ Listening skills

What You'll Need

A recording of both very slow and very fast tempos (possibilities include "Slow and Fast" from Hap Palmer's *The Feel of Music* and "Moving Slow/Moving Fast" and "Marching Slow/Marching Fast" from Rae Pica's *Preschoolers & Kindergartners Moving & Learning*), or two different recordings – one slow and one fast.

Streamers or scarves (optional)

What to Do

- ✓ Play the recording(s) you've selected, pointing out the difference between the slow and fast tempos. Can the children think of some ways each would make them feel like moving?
- ✓ Play the recording(s) again, this time challenging the children to move in a variety of ways to each tempo. Possibilities for the slow tempo include gentle swaying, walking through mud (or deep snow or peanut butter), pretending to be a turtle or a snail, and pretending to be in a film that's being played in slow motion. For the fast tempo, possibilities are running lightly (in place or around the room), skipping, pretending to be a bumblebee or hummingbird, and pretending to be a race car.

How to Ensure Success

When you first start exploring tempo with the children, you may want to act out the movements with them. This may inspire imitation but will give them a sense of security. Then, as the children gain experience, stop participating. Be sure to point out the different responses you see so they understand that it's okay to respond in diverse ways.

Be sure the pieces you choose demonstrate a vast difference between slow and fast.

Use imagery to which the children can relate.

What Else You Can Do

- ✓ Provide the children with streamers or chiffon scarves and challenge them to show you how slowly or quickly the prop can move to the music.
- ✓ Have the children select partners. Ask one partner to lead and the other to follow

114

("shadow") as the slow and fast music is played.

More Curriculum Connectors

✓ Listening skills are a necessary part of *language arts*. Also, read *The Tortoise and the Hare* for a lesson in slow and fast.

✓ Listening is related to the sense of hearing, which falls under the heading of *science*.

✓ The partner activity promotes cooperation, which is part of *social studies*, as is self-regulation.

What Else I Did

_____
_____
_____
_____
_____
_____
_____
_____
_____

Slow to Fast and Back Again

What It Teaches
- ✓ Recognition of the continuum from slow to fast (*accelerando*) and vice versa (*ritardando*)
- ✓ Experience with the movement element of time
- ✓ Physical control
- ✓ Self-regulation
- ✓ Listening skills

What You'll Need
Hand drum and mallet or a substitute

Music that accelerates or retards, or both (optional)

What to Do
- ✓ With the children sitting and listening, begin drumming very slowly. Then gradually increase your tempo until it's very fast.
- ✓ Now play a game of Follow the Leader, with you at the head of the line. Accompanying yourself with the drum (one beat for every step you take), begin to move very slowly. Gradually accelerate your tempo until you're going as fast as you want the children to go. Then begin to slow down gradually until you're back to the original speed.

How to Ensure Success
For both parts of this activity, verbally describe what you're doing as you're doing it. For example, "I'm beating the drum *very slowly* now."

Be sure your beats move from one extreme to the other gradually and steadily.

Being able to gradually increase the body's tempo to match that of the drum (or the music) is developmentally quite challenging and will require lots of repetition.

What Else You Can Do
- ✓ To make the Follow the Leader game more challenging, eventually begin to vary your movements by changing levels, directions, pathways, and, if possible, body shape.
- ✓ Once the children are familiar with this concept, have them take turns as leader.
- ✓ Try the activity to music that accelerates, retards, or does both. "Getting Fast/Getting Slow" from Rae Pica's *Preschoolers & Kindergartners Moving & Learning* is one example.

More Curriculum Connectors
- ✓ Follow the Leader is a cooperative activity, which qualifies it as *social studies*, as does the

self-regulation aspect of these activities.

✓ Being able to physically replicate what the eyes are seeing, as the children must do during Follow the Leader, is necessary in both *art* and *language arts*.

✓ Listening fits in the categories of *language arts* and *science*.

What Else I Did

_____

_____

_____

_____

_____

_____

_____

_____

Unit 16

Volume

Moving Softly/Moving Loudly

What It Teaches
- ✓ Recognition and contrast of volumes
- ✓ Experience with the movement element of force
- ✓ Listening skills

What You'll Need
Hand drum and mallet or a substitute

What to Do
- ✓ Talk to the children about very soft and very loud. What are times when they speak softly or loudly? When do they move softly or loudly?
- ✓ Ask the children to stand and move in the ways the drum makes them feel like moving. Then, alternate between very soft (light) and very loud (strong) beats.

How to Ensure Success
If the children have any trouble with this, offer suggestions as to how they could move. For example, the soft beats might inspire tiptoeing and the loud beats inspire stomping.

Be sure your beats demonstrate a vast difference between very soft and very loud. Contrasting extremes is the best way to introduce these concepts.

If you're having trouble beating the drum quietly enough, simply rub the mallet over the drumhead.

When you want the children to move softly, *speak* softly. When you want them to move strongly, talk louder.

What Else You Can Do
- ✓ Let each child have a turn with the drum, dictating the group's movement.
- ✓ As a more challenging version of this game, use just your voice to inspire soft and loud movements. How does a whisper make the children feel like moving? A shout?

More Curriculum Connectors
- ✓ Listening skills are a part of the *language arts*, as are the two different voices (whispering and shouting) suggested in "What Else You Can do."
- ✓ Listening also is related to the sense of hearing, which falls under the heading of *science*, as does the contrast in muscle tension these activities require.

What Else I Did

_____

_____

_____

_____

_____

_____

_____

_____

Moving Softly/Moving Loudly – Again

What It Teaches
- ✓ Recognition and contrast of volumes
- ✓ Experience with the movement element of force
- ✓ Listening skills

What You'll Need
One recording consisting of both very soft and very loud volumes or two different recordings – one soft and one loud (children's songs offering contrast between soft and loud include "Soft and Loud" from Hap Palmer's *The Feel of Music* and "Moving Softly/Moving Loudly" from Rae Pica's Moving & Learning Series.

Maracas or shakers (optional)

What to Do
- ✓ Play the recording(s) you've selected, pointing out the difference between the soft and loud volumes. How do the children imagine each would make them feel like moving?
- ✓ Play the recording(s) again, this time challenging them to move in a variety of ways to each volume. Possibilities for the soft volume include tiptoeing, moving as quietly as a cat, swaying gently, or "floating." For the loud volume, possibilities are stamping the feet, slapping the floor, rocking forcefully, and moving like a dinosaur.

How to Ensure Success
When you first start exploring volume with the children, act out the movements with them. This may result in imitation but will give them a sense of security. Then, as the children gain experience, stop participating. Be sure to point out the different responses you see so they understand it's okay to respond in diverse ways.

Be sure the pieces you choose demonstrate a vast difference between soft and loud.

Use imagery to which the children can relate.

What Else You Can Do
- ✓ Provide the children with maracas or shakers, and challenge them to show you how softly or loudly the prop can move to the music.
- ✓ Have the children select partners. Ask one partner to lead and the other to follow ("shadow") while the soft and loud music plays.

More Curriculum Connectors

✓ Listening skills are a component of *language arts*.
✓ Listening is related to the sense of hearing, which falls under the heading of *science*.
✓ The partner activity promotes cooperation, essential in *social studies*.

What Else I Did

_____
_____
_____
_____
_____
_____
_____
_____
_____

Soft to Loud and Back Again

What It Teaches
- ✓ Recognition of the continuum from soft to loud (*crescendo*) and vice versa (*decrescendo*)
- ✓ Experience with the movement element of force
- ✓ Physical control
- ✓ Self-regulation
- ✓ Listening skills

What You'll Need
Hand drum and mallet or a substitute

Music that increases or decreases in volume, or both (optional) (Ravel's *Bolero* is a classic example of crescendo. From Grief's *Lyric Suite*, "Norwegian Rustic March" both increases and decreases, as does "Getting Louder/Getting Softer" from Rae Pica's Moving & Learning Series.

What to Do
- ✓ With the children sitting and listening, begin drumming very softly. Then gradually increase your volume until it's very loud.
- ✓ Now play a game of Follow the Leader, with you at the head of the line. Accompanying yourself with the drum (one beat for every step you take), begin to move very softly. Gradually accelerate your volume until you're going as "loudly" as you want the children to go. Then begin to decrease your volume gradually until you're back to the original volume.

How to Ensure Success
For both parts of this activity, verbally describe what you're doing as you're doing it. For example, "I'm beating the drum *very softly* now."

Be sure your beats move from one extreme to the other gradually and steadily.

Being able to physically match the drum's (or the music's) increasing and decreasing volume is quite challenging and will require lots of repetition to ensure success.

What Else You Can Do
- ✓ To make the Follow the Leader game more challenging, eventually begin to vary your movements by changing levels, directions, pathways, and, if possible, body shape.
- ✓ Once the children are familiar with this concept, have them take turns as leader.
- ✓ Try the activity to music that increases or decreases in volume, or does both. Or play a single piece of music that you start at a very soft volume, and gradually turn up the

volume knob until the song is as loud as you want it to be.

More Curriculum Connectors

✓ Follow the Leader is a cooperative activity, which qualifies it as *social studies*, as does the self-regulation aspect of these activities.

✓ Being able to physically replicate what the eyes are seeing, as the children must do during Follow the Leader, is necessary in both *art* and *language arts*.

✓ Listening fits in the categories of *language arts* and *science*.

What Else I Did

_____

_____

_____

_____

_____

_____

_____

Unit 17
Staccato & Legato

"Pop Goes the Weasel"

What It Teaches
- ✓ Bound flow
- ✓ Listening skills

What You'll Need
A recording of "Pop Goes the Weasel" (optional)

What to Do
- ✓ Play – or hum or sing – "Pop Goes the Weasel," instructing the children to walk along with it until they hear the "pop." At the sound of the pop, have them jump into the air and then continue walking. The lyrics are:

  All around the mulberry bush
  The monkey chased the weasel
  The monkey thought it was all in fun.
  Pop goes the weasel!

  A penny for a spool of thread
  A penny for a needle
  That's the way the money goes.
  Pop goes the weasel!

- ✓ Once the children have become accustomed to this, make the activity more challenging by instructing them to jump *and* change direction when they hear the pop.

How to Ensure Success
Even if you're using a recording, sing along with it, strongly emphasizing the pop.

"Broadcast" the forthcoming pop with your posture and facial expressions.

Perform the activity with the children at first – and again when you've asked them to add the change in direction.

What Else You Can Do
- ✓ To truly interrupt the flow of movement, challenge the children to freeze in their spots when they hear the pop. They can't start moving again until the phrase ending with the word "weasel" has finished.
- ✓ Sing (or hum) the song, speeding up and slowing down indiscriminately so the children can't predict exactly when the pop will come. Also, they should match the tempo and

126

flow ("choppy" or uninterrupted) to the way you're performing the song.

More Curriculum Connectors

- ✓ Listening skills are a necessary part of *language arts*.
- ✓ Holding still, as required in the alternate activity, requires self-regulation, which is a component of *social studies*.

What Else I Did

_____
_____
_____
_____
_____
_____
_____
_____
_____

Statues

What It Teaches
- ✓ Bound flow
- ✓ Ability to differentiate between sound and silence
- ✓ Ability to stop on signal
- ✓ Self-regulation
- ✓ Listening skills

What You'll Need

Two or three songs with different musical styles (e.g., a recent Top 40 hit, a Strauss waltz, and an African or Latin piece with a strong beat)

Scarves, streamers, hoops, or foam balls (optional)

What to Do
- ✓ Explain to the children that you're going to put on a piece of music. While the music is playing, they can move in any way they want. When the music stops (you hit the pause button), they must also stop – immediately – and freeze into statues until the music begins again.
- ✓ To take the children by surprise and inspire a variety of responses, vary the time you allow them to move before stopping the music. (Don't always stop it at the end of a musical phrase.)

How to Ensure Success

Instead of asking the children to move "in the way the music makes you feel," which can be intimidating to many children, make it clear that this is a game.

Before actually beginning the game, ask the children to show you what statues look like. What are some statues they might know about (maybe the Statue of Liberty) or may have seen? Once they've assumed statue shapes, point out the tenseness of their muscles, as well as how still they are.

To expose the children to a variety of musical styles and rhythms, use a song with a different feel (a march, a waltz, rock and roll) each time you play Statues. Simply be sure the style you choose really lends itself to movement.

What Else You Can Do
- ✓ Props are an effective way to alleviate any self-consciousness children may be feeling (the focus is on the prop and not the child), and they add a whole new dimension to an activity. Give the children lightweight scarves, streamers, hoops, or foam balls, and ask

128

them to show you how the music makes the *prop* feel like moving.

✓ Once the children feel completely comfortable "improvising" to music of varying styles, make a game out of simply moving to the music (without stopping it). This will give them some experience with the element of free flow.

More Curriculum Connectors

✓ Listening is one of the four components of *language arts*.
✓ Awareness of muscle tension is part of *science* for young children.
✓ Shape is an element of *art*.
✓ The self-regulation required to hold still falls under the scope of *social studies*.

What Else I Did

_____
_____
_____
_____
_____
_____
_____
_____
_____

Bound and Free

What It Teaches

- ✓ The movement element of flow
- ✓ Listening skills

What You'll Need

Recordings of musical pieces that are examples of staccato and legato (optional)

What to Do

- ✓ Sing "Twinkle, Twinkle, Little Star" with the children. The lyrics are:

Twinkle, twinkle, little star
How I wonder what you are
Up above the world so high
Like a diamond in the sky
Twinkle, twinkle, little star
How I wonder what you are.

- ✓ Tell them you're going to sing it in different ways and that you want them to move in the way you're singing it.
- ✓ Sing the song once through in a punctuated manner, adding pauses between syllables, to portray staccato. Ask the children how the "choppiness" of the song makes them feel like moving.
- ✓ Since the song again, only this time flowing as smoothly as possible, to convey legato. Does this make the children feel like moving differently?

How to Ensure Success

Prior to facilitating this activity, challenge the children to depict certain things that move in bound and free-flowing ways. For example, you could ask them to show you how robots and butterflies move, alternating between the two. Be sure they demonstrate the muscle tension and punctuated movement of the robot and the floating easiness of the butterfly.

Demonstrate with your posture and facial expressions what you're expecting with each version of the song. For example, with the staccato version, you should be tense. With the legato, you want to show relaxed muscles.

What Else You Can Do

- ✓ Choose recordings that demonstrate both staccato and legato. For instance, portions of Haydn's *Surprise Symphony* are staccato, and "Aquarium" from Saint-Saens' *Carnival of the Animals* is an example of legato. You could play a game of Statues with the children, alternating between the two pieces.

More Curriculum Connectors

✓ Listening skills are necessary in music and in the *language arts* as well. Also, there are different book versions of "Twinkle, Twinkle, Little Star."

✓ Experience with – and awareness of – muscle tension falls under the content area of *science*.

What Else I Did

_____

_____

_____

_____

_____

_____

_____

_____

_____

Unit 18
Pitch

Do-Re-Mi

What It Teaches
- ✓ The scale
- ✓ Listening skills
- ✓ Level in space

What You'll Need
Piano, electronic keyboard, xylophone, or the scale written on a staff (optional)

What to Do
- ✓ Sing the scale to the children (do-re-mi-fa-so-la-ti-do), explaining how each successive note is higher in pitch than the previous one.
- ✓ Have the children sing the scale with you.
- ✓ Sing it again, this time asking the children to place their hands in their laps, raising them a little bit higher with each note you sing (and lowering them if you are also singing the descending scale).
- ✓ Once the children have grasped the concept, challenge them to demonstrate with their whole bodies, beginning close to the floor and getting as close to the ceiling as possible (and the reverse).

How to Ensure Success
This activity is one you'll want to perform with the children until they understand what you're expecting.

Depending on your group, limit their initial experiences to a rising scale only, and later explore it in both directions.

If it's possible to demonstrate the scale on a keyboard or on a written staff, the children will be able to *see* as well as hear the rising and descending pitches.

What Else You Can Do
- ✓ Vary this activity to also explore other concepts. The simplest variation is to change the tempo at which you sing the scale.
- ✓ Alternately sing or play in staccato or legato style.
- ✓ Add the concepts of *crescendo* and *decrescendo* by beginning at either a soft or loud volume and gradually increasing or decreasing it.
- ✓ Eventually, if the children have become very familiar with the notes of the scale and you have a keyboard or xylophone available, play the notes out of order, challenging the children to demonstrate, with their arms or the whole body, whether a note was higher or lower than the previous one.

More Curriculum Connectors

✓ The concepts of levels in space is relative to both *art* and *mathematics*.
✓ Listening skills are a component of *language arts*.

What Else I Did

_____
_____
_____
_____
_____
_____
_____
_____

High and Low

What It Teaches
- ✓ Pitch identification
- ✓ Levels in space
- ✓ Listening skills

What You'll Need
Penny whistle (optional)

Scarves or streamers (optional)

What to Do
- ✓ Make a humming sound that goes from a low pitch to a high pitch and back again (or use a penny whistle).
- ✓ This time, making either low or high humming sounds, ask the children to tell you which is high and which is low. Can they show you high and low with their body?
- ✓ Ask the children to crouch low to the floor, raising and lowering their body with your rising or descending pitch. Start by changing your pitch slowly, and increase your tempo each time you repeat it. The faster you get, the more hilarious the children will think it is!

How to Ensure Success
If necessary, participate with the children until they grasp the concept.

Begin with arms alone, before asking the children to raise and lower the whole body.

What Else You Can Do
- ✓ To make the activity more challenging, instead of moving steadily from a low to a high tone or the reverse, hum different pitches in no particular order, and ask the children to show you with their body whether the pitch you're humming is lower or higher than the previous one.
- ✓ Provide each child with a scarf or a streamer, and challenge them to move the prop at a high level when they hear a high pitch and at a low level when they hear a low pitch. Can they find different ways to move the prop?

More Curriculum Connectors
- ✓ The concept of levels in space is found in both *art* and *mathematics*. And high and low are part of Sandra Boynton's book *Opposites*.
- ✓ Listening is one of the components of *language arts*.

What Else I Did

Moving High/Moving Low

What It Teaches
- ✓ Pitch identification
- ✓ Levels and pathways
- ✓ Listening skills
- ✓ Problem solving

What You'll Need
Piano, electronic keyboard, xylophone, or other instrument(s) on which to play high and low notes

Scarves or streamers (optional)

What to Do
- ✓ With the children sitting and listening, demonstrate both high and low notes with your instrument. Ask them to close their eyes and identify which notes you play are high and which are low.
- ✓ Continue the process, this time asking the children to move about the room, finding a way to move at a low level when they hear low notes and moving at a high level when they hear high notes.

How to Ensure Success
Before conducting this activity with the accompanying sound, ask the children to think of and demonstrate some ways to move at both low and high levels. Be sure you get – and enthusiastically point out – a wide variety of responses. (Possibilities for moving at a low level include crawling, creeping, rolling, duck-walking, etc. Possibilities for moving at a high level include walking straight and tall, tiptoeing, jumping, and hopping.)

What Else You Can Do
- ✓ Provide each child with a scarf or streamer and ask the children to move the prop at a high or low level as they move around the room.
- ✓ For more of a challenge, ask the children to move the prop at the same level at which they themselves are moving (coinciding with the pitch of the notes played). For example, if they're moving at a high level, they also must be moving the prop at a high level. If they're rolling or duck-walking, for instance, they must simultaneously move the prop at a low level.
- ✓ Ask the children to each take a partner and to find a way to move at high and low levels while connected to each other (holding hands, arms linked, etc.).

More Curriculum Connectors

✓ Levels and pathways are part of both *mathematics* and *art*.
✓ Listening skills are as essential to *language arts* as they are to music.
✓ The cooperation required in the partner activity is tied to *social studies*.

What Else I Did

_____
_____
_____
_____
_____
_____
_____
_____

Unit 19

Mood

In a Mellow Mood

What It Teaches
- ✓ Association of music and mood
- ✓ Self-awareness
- ✓ Focused listening
- ✓ Relaxation

What You'll Need
A recording of a piece of music suitable for relaxation or "quiet times."

What to Do
- ✓ Play – at a reasonably low volume – the piece of music you've chosen for the children.
- ✓ Ask the children to tell you what it brings to mind.
- ✓ Challenge them to show you with their body what it makes them think of.

How to Ensure Success
If the children need encouragement, use words such as *soothing, gentle, calm,* or *easy,* to get the idea across.

If a child response in a "too energetic" way, acknowledge and validate the child's right to feel that way.

What Else You Can Do
- ✓ Suggest specific relaxation techniques while quiet music plays in the background. For instance, encourage the children to pretend to melt, to be balloons inflating and deflating (slowly inhaling and exhaling), or to be statues and ragdolls (alternately tightening and relaxing muscles).

More Curriculum Connectors
- ✓ Relaxation is a concept falling under the content area of *science*.
- ✓ Self-awareness is the beginning of *social studies* for young children.
- ✓ Focused listening is a component of *language arts*. *Five Minutes' Peace* by Jill Murphy is a fun look at the contrast between peace and lack thereof.

What Else I Did

_____
_____
_____
_____

What Mood Are You In?

What It Teaches
- ✓ Awareness and expression of emotions
- ✓ Association of feelings with the moods the music depicts
- ✓ Focused listening

What You'll Need
Two recordings – one you consider to be a very "happy" piece (such as Beethoven's "Ode to Joy" or Scott Joplin's "The Entertainer") and one that feels very "sad" to you (such as Samuel Barber's "Adagio for Strings" or a funeral march)

What to Do
- ✓ Ask the children to show you how they move when they feel happy. Challenge them to demonstrate how they move differently when they feel really sad.
- ✓ Play the song you've chosen for "happy," and ask the children to show you their happy movements as it's playing. Repeat with the "sad" song.
- ✓ Alternate between the two, not indicating which is which and inviting them to simply move in either a happy or a sad way, depending on how the music makes them feel.

How to Ensure Success
Ask the children for actual examples of times they felt really happy and others when they felt really sad. What made them feel that way? How did their body look and move each time?

What Else You Can Do
- ✓ Choose pieces of music that demonstrate other feelings children can relate to – scared (an eerie piece of electronic music), proud (a patriotic march), or silly ("Baby Elephant Walk," "Syncopated Clock," or "Itsy Bitsy Teeny Weeny Yellow Polka Dot Bikini"). Use the "What to Do" steps above to explore each of these.

More Curriculum Connectors
- ✓ Awareness and expression of feelings is an important early step in *social studies*.
- ✓ Discussing feelings and the situations that cause them involves *language arts*.
- ✓ To include both *language arts* and *art*, share with the children the book *Smiling* by Gwenyth Swain. Because it shows people smiling all over the world, it also incorporates *social studies*.

What Else I Did

_____

_____

_____

_____

_____

_____

_____

_____

In the Mood

What It Teaches
- ✓ Awareness and expression of emotions
- ✓ Recognition of the moods expressed by music
- ✓ Listening skills

What You'll Need
A selection of recordings depicting different moods the children can relate to, such as happy, sad, proud, tired, scared, silly, or mad (possibilities include marches for proud; Bach's "Musette in D-Major" for happy; Brahms' "Lullaby" for tired; and the theme music from a science fiction movie for scared)

Various instruments and/or props (optional)

What to Do
- ✓ Play one of the pieces you've chosen, and ask the children to move in whatever way they'd like to move to the music. After a while, repeat with another selection.
- ✓ Repeat this process, playing the pieces in a random order, always asking the children to move in a way the music makes them want to move.

How to Ensure Success
Children are often more sensitive than adults to the feelings conveyed by music, so they may not necessarily have the same reaction to a piece of music that you do. They may even respond in different ways from each other! That's fine. The idea is for them to react to the music in whatever way it makes *them* feel. Let them know it's acceptable for them to respond individually.

What Else You Can Do
- ✓ Play a game of Statues using a variety of pieces with different moods, and ask the children to freeze in a "statue" pose that represents the mood they're portraying.
- ✓ Have a variety of music instruments and/or props available for the children to choose from (several of each). When a piece of music is played, have each child select an instrument or a prop to use that he or she thinks is most suitable for the mood of the music.

More Curriculum Connectors
- ✓ Awareness and expression of emotion are part of *social studies*.
- ✓ The focused listening required is an element of *language arts*. Share with your group *The Feelings Book* by Todd Parr.

What Else I Did

_____

_____

_____

_____

_____

_____

_____

_____

Unit 20

Rhythm

Body Rhythm

What It Teaches
- ✓ An introduction to rhythm
- ✓ Problem solving

What You'll Need
No equipment or materials needed

What to Do
- ✓ Challenge the children to discover at least two different sounds they can create with their hands.
- ✓ Ask them what other body parts they can use to create sound. (Possibilities include feet, tongue, and teeth.)
- ✓ Ask them to move around the room, accompanying themselves with some of these sounds. Can they use different parts of the room (floor, walls, white board) to create new sounds?

How to Ensure Success
Children love to make noise, and making noise with their body is a great introduction to rhythm. You may have to reassure them that it's really okay for them to be making noise during the times when you say it's okay.

Encourage the creation of new and different sounds by suggesting words such as *clap, stamp, stomp, flick, scuff, shuffle,* or *pat.*

What Else You Can Do
- ✓ What different, accompanying sounds can the children find outdoors? Possibilities include stamping on pavement, shuffling through fallen leaves, banging rocks together, and tapping with a stick.
- ✓ Talk to the children about the sounds of a cough, sneeze, yawn, hiccup, giggle, and snore. Ask them to show you how each sound makes their bodies move. Ask them either to incorporate the sound into their movements or to perform silently. Challenge them to do each movement more than once.

More Curriculum Connectors
- ✓ Investigating the possibilities for moving and creating sounds with different body parts is a great *science* experiment for young children.
- ✓ The concept of *how many* falls under the heading of *mathematics.*
- ✓ Attaching meaning to the words in the extension activity incorporates *language arts.* To

combine *language arts*, *social studies*, and *art*, read *I See the Rhythm*, written by Toyomi Igus and illustrated by Michele Wood, with the children.

What Else I Did

_____

_____

_____

_____

_____

_____

_____

_____

Match the Movement

What It Teaches
- ✓ Awareness of rhythm
- ✓ Listening skills

What You'll Need
Hand drum and mallet or appropriate substitutes (such as a coffee can with a plastic lid and a wooden spoon)

What to Do
- ✓ Ask the children to walk around the room in any way they like.
- ✓ With your drum, beat out a rhythmic pattern that matches their movements. When they change their movements (for example, from small to big steps or from light to heavy steps), change the drumbeat to match those movements.
- ✓ Repeat the process with other locomotor skills (running, galloping, jumping, etc.).

How to Ensure Success
Very young children aren't developmentally ready to match their movements to an imposed beat. Synchronizing your instrumental accompaniment to *their* rhythm automatically sets them up for success. They'll be excited to realize that they're responsible for the rhythms you're creating!

If the children don't vary their movements on their own, suggest that they change their tempo, force, or pathways.

What Else You Can Do
- ✓ Let the drum dictate the kind of movement the children should perform. For instance, swish the mallet quietly around the drumskin to inspire soft movements, or beat the drum loudly and slowly for giant steps. Tap the side of the drum with the stick itself to inspire light, percussive movement. (Be sure that you're not expecting the children to be able to move "at one" with the beat.)
- ✓ With just a little bit of experience with the preceding game, have the children take responsibility for the instrumental accompaniment. Give each child a turn to control the drum, and watch their eyes light up as they realize they power they have in their hands!

More Curriculum Connectors
- ✓ Listening skills are a component of *language arts*.
- ✓ If possible, use a variety of percussion instruments originating from different parts of the world to contribute to the children's multicultural education, which falls under the

content area of *social studies*.

What Else I Did

_____
_____
_____
_____
_____
_____
_____
_____

Echo

What It Teaches
- ✓ An introduction to beat groupings (meters)
- ✓ Counting
- ✓ Listening skills

What You'll Need
No equipment or materials needed

What to Do
- ✓ Explain to the children that you're going to clap a certain number of times and, after you've finished, you want them to clap, too – to echo what they heard you do.
- ✓ Clap and count out a small group of beats (1-2 or 1-2-3, for example).
- ✓ Continue the process, clapping and counting, with the children echoing you.

How to Ensure Success
When you first perform this activity, repeat each beat grouping at least once to give children a second chance to hear it and repeat it successfully.

Start with a small number of beats – not exceeding four to begin.

Clap and count at a slow to moderate tempo until the children are ready for a faster pace.

What Else You Can Do
- ✓ To create variety, repeat or "mix and match" groupings. For example, clap and count 1-2, 1-2, or try something like 1-2, 1-2-3.
- ✓ To make the game more challenging, clap without counting aloud.
- ✓ Once the children are comfortable clapping various beat groupings, ask them to stand and try stepping in place to each beat. You may have to return to a slower tempo for a while.

More Curriculum Connectors
- ✓ Counting, of course, is a *mathematics* function.
- ✓ Listening is a component of *language arts*.
- ✓ The children in your class for whom English is a second language could be asked to teach everyone how to count to four in their first language to incorporate the *social studies* concept of different languages in different countries.

What Else I Did

_____
_____
_____
_____
_____
_____
_____
_____

Common Meters

What It Teaches
- ✓ An introduction to meters commonly used in Western music
- ✓ Appreciation for a variety of music
- ✓ Listening skills
- ✓ Practice with various movement skills

What You'll Need
Recordings of music in 2/4, 3/4, and 4/4 meters

Recordings in 6/8, 5/4, 5/8, or 7/8 meters (optional)

What to Do
- ✓ Choose a piece of music with a 2/4 meter (for example, a march or a polka) and play a little bit of it for the children to hear.
- ✓ Start the piece again, and encourage the children to try your suggested movements to accompany it. Possibilities for 2/4 include clapping 1-2, marching, stamping feet, jumping, and hopping.
- ✓ Repeat the process with a piece in 3/4 (a waltz is most common). Suggested movements might include clapping 1-2-3, swaying, and swinging the body or body parts (arms, legs, head).
- ✓ Repeat the process with a piece in a 4/4 meter (rock and roll and many Top 40 songs are performed in this most common meter). Movement possibilities include clapping 1-2-3-4, jogging, stamping feet, and bouncing up and down.

How to Ensure Success
Depending on the children's developmental level and the amount of time available, extend these activities over several days, perhaps concentrating on one meter per session.

Have the children simply move in any way they want to each meter before asking them to try your suggestions.

Perform the suggested movements with the children at first.

What Else You Can Do
- ✓ For more of a challenge, explore a 6/8 meter (six eighth-notes to the measure, found often in folk songs and some marches). Movement possibilities include clapping 1-2, marching, rocking, and moving the head from side to side.
- ✓ Also challenging are pieces in meters less common in the United States, such as 5/4, 5/8,

and 7/8. Invite the children to move in any way they want to these pieces.

✓ Play a game of Statues, alternating among the various meters.

More Curriculum Connectors

✓ Listening skills are necessary to *language arts*.
✓ Using pieces representative of different ethnicities contributes to multicultural education, a part of *social studies*.
✓ If you count claps you'll be incorporating an aspect of *mathematics*.

What Else I Did

_____

_____

_____

_____

_____

_____

_____

_____

_____

Section Five

SCIENCE

The word *science* reminds many adults of topics such as chemistry, physics, biology, botany, and astronomy. We might imagine men and women in laboratory coats, poring over facts and figures or measuring strange concoctions into test tubes and beakers. Because none of this is relevant in the lives of young children, you might wonder – rightly – how science fits into the early childhood curriculum.

The fact is that science is also about exploration, investigation, problem solving, and discovery – all of which *are* relevant for young children. A child's whole life, from the very beginning, is exploring, investigating, solving problems, and discovering!

The principal difference between these two views of science is that much of the former deals with the theoretical and the abstract, while the latter, as far as young children are concerned, deals with the concrete and the tangible – with what can be readily observed. For example, children discover which objects will float or sink by actually placing objects in water. They discover a different type of floating by blowing bubbles through a wand and watching them drift through the air. Balls, however, will not float when sent into the air; this is because of gravity, a concept the children may not grasp but one they can witness firsthand.

Science for young children is learning by doing – just as movement is.

Many themes typically explored in early childhood settings fall under the science category, including themes such as the human body (body parts and their functions, hygiene, and nutrition), seasons, and animals. These are covered in the lesson plans that follow, as are specific scientific concepts appropriate for exploration with young children.

Of course, any time children perform movements – locomotor, nonlocomotor, manipulative, gymnastic, or dance – they are learning something about the functions of the human body. It could be said, therefore, that whenever children are moving, they're also learning something about science!

Unit 21

My Body

Simon Says

What It Teaches
- ✓ Body-part identification
- ✓ Listening skills

What You'll Need
No equipment or materials needed

What to Do
- ✓ Arrange the children into two groups – in either circles or lines.
- ✓ Explain that you're going to pretend to be someone called "Simon," and when you say "Simon says...," they're to do whatever Simon has asked them to do. But if you tell them to do something without first saying "Simon says," they shouldn't do it! If they do, they move to the other line or circle.
- ✓ "Simon's" commands might include challenges such as touching different body parts (toes, shoulders, elbows, etc.), blinking eyes, wiggling fingers or noses, waving hands, puckering lips, bending knees, standing on one foot, and giving themselves a hug.

How to Ensure Success
If the children are too young to grasp the concept of Simon, use the name of a favorite stuffed animal or character.

Performing the action with the children at first almost guarantees success, because people have been shown to respond better to visual signals than audible signals.

Eliminating the elimination process pretty much ensures the children won't feel badly about moving without Simon having said they could. Just make sure they realize that moving from one group to the other is part of the fun too!

What Else You Can Do
- ✓ Play a game called Show Me, in which you call our various body parts and actions you want the children to display. Games such as the ones suggested in this activity can't be repeated too often! Body-part identification is an important first step in movement and physical education, and once children enter elementary school, they won't have many opportunities to partake in self-awareness activities.
- ✓ Other body parts activities include Head, Bellies, Toes and Head, Shoulders, Knees, and Toes.

More Curriculum Connectors

✓ Listening skills are essential to both *language arts* and *music*.

✓ Self-awareness is the first step in *social studies* for young children. You might include a multicultural element by saying the body parts in different languages. Do any of your children know the words for these body parts in another language?

What Else I Did

_____

_____

_____

_____

_____

_____

_____

_____

_____

Hands Down

What It Teaches
- ✓ Body awareness
- ✓ Self-expression

What You'll Need
No equipment or materials needed

What to Do
- ✓ Have a discussion with the children about their hands. What are the various parts that make up a hand? Have they ever thought about all the things their hands do for them?
- ✓ Ask them to pretend to do a variety of things with their hands and to think about the many ways they must move their hands to accomplish these tasks. Possible challenges include pretending to wave hello or goodbye, play the piano or guitar, brush teeth, brush hair, wash the face, button clothes, pull up a zipper, bounce a ball, dial a phone, tie shoes, and turn the pages of a book.

How to Ensure Success
There is no wrong way to respond here, but if it makes the children more comfortable, demonstrate the activities when you first begin playing this game.

Use only challenges the children can relate to, given their age and experience, to ensure success. For instance, a preschooler in New York City might be able to demonstrate hailing a cab, but a child raised in the suburbs or a rural area would be completely unfamiliar with this action.

What Else You Can Do
- ✓ Play a game of Feet First, in which you ask the children to demonstrate all the possible things feet can do. Possibilities include walking, climbing stairs or ladders, jogging, jumping, hopping, tiptoeing, ice skating, and kicking a ball. This is a wonderful way to get them moving!

More Curriculum Connectors
- ✓ Self-awareness and self-expression are also components of *social studies*.
- ✓ Read *Here Are My Hands* by Bill Martin, Jr. and John Archambault to incorporate *language arts*.

What Else I Did

_____

_____

_____

_____

_____

_____

_____

_____

Move It!

What It Teaches
- ✓ Body awareness
- ✓ Practice with motor skills
- ✓ Listening skills

What You'll Need
No equipment or materials needed

What to Do
- ✓ Tell the children you're going to call out one way of moving after another and they're to move that way until they hear you say "Freeze!"
- ✓ Call out various locomotor skills – walk, run, jump, leap, gallop, hop, slide, and skip – varying the amount of time you have them move and freeze.

How to Ensure Success
Call out only those skills you're sure all the children can execute.

Let the children dictate the length of this game. If you see them begin to tire, bring the game to an end.

What Else You Can Do
- ✓ Once the children can perform many locomotor skills well on their own, play a "numbers" game. Challenge them to perform each skill as you call it out, as before. But when they hear you call out a number, have them connect to enough other children to make up that number, and continue performing the skill. For example, if they are galloping and you call out the number "three," they will each have to find two other children, make a connection of some kind (hands held, elbows linked, etc.), and continue galloping.
- ✓ Play the original game with nonlocomotor skills – bend, stretch, sit, shake, turn, rock, sway, swing, and twist – challenging the children to find many ways to perform each skill.
- ✓ When the children are developmentally ready, call out *combinations* of skills, beginning with two at a time. For example, challenge them to perform two different locomotor skills, one after the other (for example, walk-jump), or combine a locomotor skill with a nonlocomotor skill (for example, walk-stretch).

More Curriculum Connectors
- ✓ Listening skills are linked to both *language arts* and *music*. Incorporate more music by using movement-inspiring albums such as *Mr. Al Sings and Moves*, Greg and Steve's *Kids in Motion*, or Rae Pica and Richard Gardzina's *Wiggle, Giggle, & Shake*.

- ✓ Performing locomotor skills while "connected" to others is a cooperative activity and therefore falls under the category of *social studies*.
- ✓ Having to count the number of children with whom they connect – or the number of ways you can perform each nonlocomotor skill – is a *mathematics* concept.

What Else I Did

_____
_____
_____
_____
_____
_____
_____
_____

Common Senses

What It Teaches
- ✓ Self-awareness
- ✓ Identification of and appreciation for the various senses
- ✓ Self-expression

What You'll Need
No equipment or materials needed

What to Do
- ✓ Talk to the children about the things they most like to taste, smell, hear, feel, and see. What things do they like least?
- ✓ Using some of their responses, ask them now to show you how their face and/or body moves in reaction to these tastes, smells, sounds, textures, and sights. For example, what happens when they taste a sour lemon, a very bubbly drink, peanut butter, or their favorite ice cream; smell a skunk, cookies baking, onions, or flowers; hear a loud noise or their favorite music; wear a "scratchy" sweater, feel their pet's fur, or accidentally touch something hot; or look for something lost on the floor or up at the stars at night?

How to Ensure Success
If you think exploring all this territory at one time will be overwhelming for the children, focus on one sense per session.

If the children need extra "coaching," use descriptive words to help them respond. For example, ask if a sour lemon makes them feel like puckering up their mouth or if they describe the scratchy sweater as being itchy or pinchy.

What Else You Can Do
- ✓ The listening activities in the Language Arts section would fit in with your exploration of the sense of hearing.
- ✓ Ask the children to depict the shape or movement of some of the sources of these tastes, smells, sounds, textures, and sights (such as a bubbly drink, a skunk, a hot iron).

More Curriculum Connectors
- ✓ Self-awareness is part of *social studies*.
- ✓ Texture is a component of *art*, as is the ability to translate what one sees into another means of expression.
- ✓ If you use descriptive words, you're incorporating *language arts*. To include both language arts and *art*, share Aliki's *My Five Senses* with the children.

What Else I Did

_____
_____
_____
_____
_____
_____
_____
_____

What It Teaches
- ✓ Relaxation
- ✓ Proper breathing and consideration of the lungs
- ✓ Self-control
- ✓ Contraction and release of the muscles

What You'll Need
Balloon (optional)

What to Do
- ✓ Talk to the children about balloons and what's meant by inflating and deflating. Do inflation and deflation happen quickly or slowly?
- ✓ Ask them to imagine they're each a balloon – in whatever color they choose. Have the children pretend to "inflate" by inhaling and then "deflate" by exhaling – slowly!
- ✓ Repeat the activity a couple of times until the children have achieved a certain level of relaxation.

How to Ensure Success
Demonstrate inflation and deflation to the children with an actual balloon to help make the image more vivid.

Before "inflating," ask the children to start off in a small shape, as close to the floor as possible. They're then going to get bigger, just as balloons do when inflating. While deflating, they should get smaller and smaller, just as balloons do.

Encourage the children to inflate by inhaling through their nose and deflate by exhaling through their mouth so they can learn this important relaxation technique.

What Else You Can Do
- ✓ To inspire relaxation through contraction and release of the muscles, play Statues/Rag Dolls. For this activity, ask them first to look like a statue (explain that statues are very stiff). Then ask them to show you what a ragdoll looks like. Alternate between the two images, finishing with the ragdoll.
- ✓ "Melting" is a wonderful slow-motion activity that helps the children unwind. Talk to them about how slowly ice cream cones, snow sculptures, and ice cubes melt. Ask them to stand and demonstrate one of these possibilities.

More Curriculum Connectors

✓ Because *music* is mood-altering, it offers great potential for relaxation. Accompany any of the activities with pieces recorded especially for resting and quiet times (many children's albums are written just for this purpose) or with classical or New Age compositions that you've found to be soothing.

✓ The quantitative concepts of *bigger* and *smaller* are part of *mathematics*.

✓ Read Genichiro Yagyu's *The Holes in Your Nose* to incorporate *language arts*.

What Else I Did

_____

_____

_____

_____

_____

_____

_____

_____

_____

Unit 22

Hygiene

Rub-a-Dub-Dub

What It Teaches
- ✓ Cleanliness can be fun
- ✓ Body-part identification

What You'll Need
No equipment or materials needed

What to Do
- ✓ Talk to the children about washing up. What are the times when they should always wash their hands (after going to the bathroom, after coughing or sneezing, before eating)? Why is it important? What is their favorite color of washcloth at home? Do they have special toys they take into the tub with them? What kind of soap do they use?
- ✓ Ask them to show you how they would wash various body parts – the face, hands, elbows, knees, tummy, back, neck, feet. Stress realistic actions.
- ✓ Accompany the activity with the nursery rhyme, "Rub-a-Dub-Dub," substituting the word "kids" for "men." Or, to the melody of "The Mulberry Bush," sing
  > *This is the way we wash our [hands],*
  > *Wash our [hands], wash our [hands].*
  > *This is the way we wash our [hands]*
  > *Early in the morning.*

How to Ensure Success
There's no way to get this activity wrong! Be sure you ask the children to wash the body parts you know they can readily identify.

What Else You Can Do
- ✓ When the children are ready, make the activity more challenging by including other body parts such as wrists, shins, throat, and temples.
- ✓ Introduce – or give the children greater experience with – laterality by asking them to "wash" parts on just one side of the body, for example, invite them to wash the *left* knee or the *right* foot.

More Curriculum Connectors
- ✓ Using the nursery rhyme involves *language arts*, and using a song includes language arts and *music*.
- ✓ *Scrubba Dub*, written by Nancy Van Laan and illustrated by Bernadette Pons, is a great choice to accompany these activities.

What Else I Did

_____

_____

_____

_____

_____

_____

_____

_____

Hair Care

What It Teaches
✓ The various aspects of hair care

What You'll Need
No equipment or materials needed

What to Do
✓ Talk to the children about various aspects of hair care. What's their favorite shampoo? Do they brush or comb their hair? How many in the room have long hair and how many have short hair? Are their children who wear their hair in braids, plaits, or beaded?
✓ Ask the children to demonstrate the motions involved in any or all of the above hair-related tasks.
✓ Challenge them to pretend to be the following: shampoo bubbling, a comb or brush running down a long mane of hair, running water, scissors cutting hair, and a blow dryer.

How to Ensure Success
Expect as many responses to your challenges as there are children. You'll be amazed at how many ways they can find to "be" water, for example.

What Else You Can Do
✓ Ask the children to show you all the things hairstylists and barbers do in their work. (Offer verbal assistance if they get stuck.)

More Curriculum Connectors
✓ Counting the number of children with short and long hair constitutes *math*.
✓ Pretending to be hairstylists and barbers is an exploration of occupations, which falls under the heading of *social studies*.
✓ Read *I Love My Hair*, by Natasha Tarpley and illustrated by E.B. Lewis, to include *language arts*, *art*, and *social studies*. Another book possibility is *The Girl Who Wouldn't Brush Her Hair* by Kate Bernheimer.

What Else I Did

_____
_____
_____
_____
_____

A Bite Out of Life

What It Teaches
✓ Appreciation of dental care

What You'll Need
Toothbrush, floss, and toothpaste, or pictures of them (optional)

What to Do
✓ Discuss dental care with the children. What colors are their toothbrushes at home? What's their favorite toothpaste? How many times a day do they brush? Do they know what flossing is?
✓ Ask them to demonstrate the following possibilities: the shape of a toothbrush, the motion of a battery-powered toothbrush, the shape of a piece of floss (how long can they make themselves?), the motion of floss sliding between the teeth, how wide they can open their mouth, toothpaste coming out of the tube, the toothpaste tube being squeezed, and the toothpaste tube being rolled up from the bottom.

How to Ensure Success
Have the preceding items (or pictures of them) available for the children to see.

Give verbal encouragement. For example, tell the children a battery-powered toothbrush *vibrates*, which is like very fast shaking.

What Else You Can Do
✓ Challenge the children to discover how many different sounds they can make with their teeth, and then accompany their sounds with movements. (Explain that their teeth can be like rhythm instruments.)

More Curriculum Connectors
✓ Taking on various shapes with the body falls under the heading of *art*.
✓ Creating sound is part of *music*. To add more music, play Raffi's "Brush Your Teeth," from *Singable Songs for the Very Young*, and "Brush Away," from Volume II of Hap Palmer's *Learning Basic Skills Through Music*.
✓ To include *math*, ask the children to count the different sounds they can make with their teeth. Also, can they use their tongue to count their *teeth*?
✓ To incorporate *language arts*, read *How Many Teeth?* written by Paul Showers and illustrated by True Kelly.

What Else I Did

_____

_____

_____

_____

_____

_____

_____

_____

Laundry Day

What It Teaches
- ✓ Appreciation for care of clothing
- ✓ Experience with household machines

What You'll Need
No equipment or materials needed

What to Do
- ✓ Talk to the children about washing machines, dryers, ironing, and other elements of clothes care. Do they know the difference between a gentle cycle and a spin cycle? Does the washing machine at home or at their laundromat open from the top or from the front? How about the dryer? Does the dryer have a window in its door so they can watch the clothes go around and around?
- ✓ Invite the children to demonstrate the actions of a washing machine, including possibilities such as having its lid opened, filling up with water, churning on the gentle or spin cycle, and slowing down and coming to a stop.
- ✓ How can they demonstrate clothes being tumbled in a dryer?

How to Ensure Success
Discussing all these elements in advance can help the children more accurately portray the imagery here, but expect them to relate to the images in their own individual ways.

If some children in your group don't have a washer and dryer at home, include a discussion of laundromats.

What Else You Can Do
- ✓ Ask the children to show you the shapes of various articles of clothing – for example, a shirt, pants, a sock, scarf, or hat. Introduce the children to the clothing of other cultures, such as a sari or a kilt.
- ✓ Invite the children to demonstrate the difference between clothes being tumble-dried and those drying outside on a line.
- ✓ Ask the children to reenact the entire process of dirty clothes being tossed into a hamper to being washed, dried, and ironed – either as the person doing the chores or from the clothes' point of view!

More Curriculum Connectors
- ✓ Machinery is another aspect of *science*.
- ✓ Shape is a component of the content area of *art*.

✓ To incorporate *music*, ask the children to sing "This is the way we [wash] our clothes" (to the tune of "The Mulberry Bush") while they demonstrate their actions.
✓ Including the clothing of other cultures brings in *social studies*.

What Else I Did

_____
_____
_____
_____
_____
_____
_____
_____

Unit 23
Nutrition

Eat Your Fruits and Veggies

What It Teaches
- ✓ Familiarity with fruits and vegetables as healthy foods
- ✓ The movement element of shape
- ✓ The concept of size

What You'll Need
Various fruits and vegetables or pictures of them

What to Do
- ✓ Talk to the children about different fruits and vegetables, and show pictures of as many as possible. What are their favorite fruits and vegetables? How do they like to eat them? Explain that we're supposed to eat several servings of each every day because they're an important source of "fuel" for the body.
- ✓ Ask the children to demonstrate the shapes of various fruits and vegetables with their body or body parts. Possibilities include bananas, grapes, oranges, pumpkins, (doing these three consecutively helps them consider the concept of size), pears, zucchini or squash, and carrots.

How to Ensure Success
Have pictures – or the actual fruits and vegetables – available to greatly contribute to both the discussion and the demonstration.

Be sure to talk about how some foods have the same shape (grapes, oranges, and pumpkins, for example) but differ in size.

What Else You Can Do
- ✓ Talk to the children about the "before" and "after" of some fruits and vegetables. Ask the children to depict them for you. Possibilities include an apple hanging on a tree/applesauce simmering on the stove, a grape/grape jelly being spread, an orange being peeled/orange juice being poured, a potato being peeled/a potato being mashed. (If possible, *prepare* some fruits and vegetables so the children can get tangible evidence of raw versus cooked. Then have a tasting party!)

More Curriculum Connectors

✓ The element of shape is a major factor in *art*.

✓ The concept of size is part of *mathematics*.

✓ Read *Oliver's Vegetables* by Vivian French to incorporate *language arts*.

What Else I Did

_____

_____

_____

_____

_____

_____

_____

_____

_____

What It Teaches
- ✓ Awareness of grains (one of the food groups)
- ✓ The movement element of force
- ✓ The movement element of shape

What You'll Need
A variety of pastas in different shapes; rice (both optional)

What to Do
- ✓ Talk to the children about spaghetti. What shape is it? What is it like when it's uncooked? What happens when it's placed in boiling water? What happens if cooked spaghetti is left on the plate too long? Is it hard or soft then? What shape is it then?
- ✓ Challenge the children to portray spaghetti in its various stages: uncooked and in a box, coming out of the box, being placed in boiling water, being stirred, being placed on a plate, and being left out and drying up.

How to Ensure Success
Be as specific as possible in your discussion to contribute to the success of this venture.

If possible, cook spaghetti in the classroom prior to participating in these activities, to contribute to the children's understanding and knowledge.

As the children are depicting the various stages, provide additional verbal help, using words such as *stiff*, *loose*, *limp*, and *crunchy*.

What Else You Can Do
- ✓ Talk about – or display – pastas of varying shapes (examples: rotini, spiral, bowtie, shells, lasagna, ravioli). Challenge the children to show you these different shapes with their bodies.
- ✓ Rice is another component of this food group and is eaten throughout the world. Talk to the children about rice in its precooked and cooked states (demonstrate if possible and invite them to depict the transformation from small, hard morsel to soft, plumped rice. Be sure they understand this is a *slow* process.

More Curriculum Connectors
- ✓ The movement element of force involves muscle tension, an aspect of *science*.
- ✓ Shape is a component of the content area of *art*.
- ✓ *Everybody Cooks Rice* offers a *language arts* component, as well as *social studies*, because

the main character roams her neighborhood and discovers different families from different countries, all cooking with rice.

   ✓ The measuring involved in cooking pasta and/or rice is a concept in *mathematics*.

What Else I Did

_____

_____

_____

_____

_____

_____

_____

_____

Bread, Bread, Bread

What It Teaches
✓ Awareness of bread and bread making

What You'll Need
No equipment or materials needed

What to Do
✓ Talk to the children about bread making *before* the advent of bread machines, reviewing the various steps involved (stirring the ingredients to make the dough, and then kneading, rolling, shaping, and baking the dough).
✓ To the tune of "The Mulberry Bush," sing "This is the way we stir (knead, roll, shape, bake) the dough," accompanying each verse with the appropriate motions.

How to Ensure Success
During the discussion, be sure the children fully understand the concepts involved.

If necessary, perform the actions with the children at first.

If possible, make bread in the classroom!

What Else You Can Do
✓ Invite the children to demonstrate what it would be like to *be* the dough as it's stirred, kneaded, rolled out, shaped, and baked. (What happens when it's baked? Answer: It rises some more and becomes firmer.)
✓ Ask the children to show you the shapes of their favorite types of breads. These might include muffins, pretzels, bagels, and others.

More Curriculum Connectors
✓ Accompanying the children's actions with a song incorporates *music*. Creating new lyrics involves *language arts*.
✓ To further incorporate *language arts*, read *Bread, Bread, Bread* by Ann Morris and/or *Everybody Bakes Bread* by Norah Dooley. Both books are multicultural in nature (*social studies*).
✓ Exploring the shapes of various breads is an *art* concept.

What Else I Did

_____

_____

_____

_____

_____

_____

_____

_____

Unit 24
Seasons

What It Teaches
- ✓ Awareness of the fall season as experienced in many parts of the world
- ✓ Awareness of weather concepts
- ✓ The movement element of force

What You'll Need
Parachute and cut out (or real) leaves (optional)

What to Do
- ✓ Talk to the children about how the leaves change colors and then fall from the trees during autumn in many parts of the country. How do they fall – heavily, hitting the ground with a lot of force, or lightly, taking a while to gently descend to earth?
- ✓ Also ask them to tell you how the weather changes. Does it get warmer or colder in the fall? What's the wind like in autumn?
- ✓ Invite the children to depict leaves falling from the trees while you act as the wind, "blowing them around." Challenge them to "fly" higher and lower and to spin and swirl.

How to Ensure Success
Encourage the children to move as lightly as possible by using words such as *gentle, easy*, and *drifting*.

What Else You Can Do
- ✓ Scatter cut out, colored leaves (or actual fallen leaves) on a parachute the children are holding. How can the children make the leaves "fall to the ground?"
- ✓ Challenge the children to demonstrate the actions involved in certain autumn activities, such as raking leaves and then jumping in the pile. How would picking apples look different from picking pumpkins?

More Curriculum Connectors
- ✓ The movement element of force involves muscle tension, an aspect of *science*, as is the concept of cause and effect (between the wind and the leaves).
- ✓ Positional concepts including *higher* and *lower* relate to both *art* and *mathematics*.
- ✓ The book *Leaves* by David Ezra Stein incorporates *language arts*.

What Else I Did

_____
_____

What It Teaches

- ✓ Awareness of the winter season as experienced in many parts of the world
- ✓ Familiarity with the concepts of *small* and *large* and the gradations in between
- ✓ The movement element of time
- ✓ Experience with relaxation

What You'll Need

A large thermometer (optional)
Parachute and cotton balls or Styrofoam peanuts (optional)

What to Do

- ✓ Talk to the children about building snowpeople. Have they ever made one? Discuss the fact that snowpeople start with a single snowball and then gradually increase in size.
- ✓ Challenge the children to show you what they would look like if they were each a snowball. Ask them to imagine they're being built into snowpeople, gradually getting bigger and bigger.
- ✓ When the snowpeople are as big as they can get, ask them to imagine that the sun is shining on them, causing them to slowly melt – until they're nothing but puddles on the ground.

How to Ensure Success

Because moving very slowly doesn't come naturally to most children, encourage them to do so – both when they're growing and when they're melting.

What Else You Can Do

- ✓ When the children are ready to work in partners, have them take turns shaping each other into "snow sculptures."
- ✓ Ask the children to demonstrate what their hands do when they're very cold. How do their bodies look? Ask them to show you how they shiver – just a little and then very hard.
- ✓ Invite the children to demonstrate the actions involved in a variety of winter sports. Possibilities include skating, cross-country skiing, downhill skiing, playing hockey, and snowshoeing.
- ✓ Talk to the children about falling temperatures in the winter. Show them a thermometer, explaining that the liquid is called *mercury*, and it falls as the temperature does. Invite them to pretend they're mercury at the warmest point in the day. At what level would they be? As the sun sets and the temperature drops, so does the mercury. How can they demonstrate that? Would the movement be fast or slow?
- ✓ Place several handfuls of cotton balls or Styrofoam peanuts on a parachute and

challenge the children to create a "snowstorm."

More Curriculum Connectors

- ✓ The concept of size is part of *mathematics*.
- ✓ The cooperation involved in the partner activity is relevant to *social studies*.
- ✓ The partner activity also involves the element of shape, which is part of *art*.
- ✓ To incorporate *language arts*, read Anne and Harlow Rockwell's *The First Snowfall*.

What Else I Did

_____
_____
_____
_____
_____
_____
_____
_____
_____

Spring

What It Teaches
- ✓ Awareness of the spring season as experienced in many parts of the world
- ✓ Awareness of the cycle of life
- ✓ The movement element of time
- ✓ The concept of size

What You'll Need
No equipment or materials needed

What to Do
- ✓ Talk to the children about the planting of seeds in the spring. What happens as the weather warms up and the ground (seeds) receive both rain and sunshine? Do the resulting flowers and plants grow quickly or slowly?
- ✓ Invite the children to imagine they're tiny seeds under the earth. With you alternately acting as the sun and the rain, the "seeds" begin to slowly grow into beautiful plants and flowers.
- ✓ What would the plants and flowers look like if a warm spring breeze were blowing them? What if there was a lot of rain and it made the plants and flowers "droopy?"

How to Ensure Success
Encourage the children to grow as slowly as possible by reminding them that it takes a long time for seeds to become plants and flowers.

What Else You Can Do
- ✓ Spring cleaning is as much a part of the season as any climate changes. Talk to the children about spring cleaning, and then ask them to demonstrate the actions involved in the various tasks. Possibilities include washing windows, painting, shampooing the carpet, shaking out rugs, and putting away winter clothes.

More Curriculum Connectors
- ✓ The concept of size is relevant to both *art* and *mathematics*.
- ✓ Introduce the spring cleaning activity by discussing the work of homemakers and professional housecleaners (or painters), thus initiating a discussion of occupations, which falls under the heading of *social studies*.
- ✓ Accompany the principal activity with Eric Carle's *The Tiny Seed*, to incorporate *language arts*.

What Else I Did

_____
_____
_____
_____
_____
_____
_____
_____

Summer

What It Teaches
- ✓ Awareness of the summer season
- ✓ Awareness of the rising and setting of the sun
- ✓ Introduction to geographical directions
- ✓ The movement element of time
- ✓ The concepts of up and down
- ✓ Levels in space

What You'll Need
A large thermometer (optional)

What to Do
- ✓ Talk to the children about summer. What do they like best about it? What's the weather like during the summer?
- ✓ Explain, as simply as possible, that one of the things they might notice about summer is how long the days stay light. That means that the sun rises earlier in the morning and sets later in the evening. Have they ever watched the sun rise or set?
- ✓ Point out the four different geographical directions to the children, explaining that the sun rises in the east and sets in the west.
- ✓ Ask the children to line up side by side on the side of the room you've designated as the east, and to crouch down low, waiting for the time when the sun will rise. At a signal from you, they begin to *slowly* rise and move across the "sky" (the room), then "set" in the west. Can they depict the sun "shining" as they move?

How to Ensure Success
Encourage the children to move as slowly as possible across the room by reminding them of how many hours it takes for the sun to rise in the east and set in the west.

What Else You Can Do
- ✓ Talk to the children about different summer sports and activities. Ask them to demonstrate the actions involved in some of them. Possibilities include swimming, tennis, bicycle riding, roller skating, fishing, going on a picnic, and golfing.
- ✓ Talk to the children about rising temperatures in the summer. Show them a thermometer and explain how the mercury rises as the temperature rises. Invite them to start off very low to the floor, pretending to be the mercury on a very cool morning. As the sun rises and the day warms up, they rise too.

More Curriculum Connectors

✓ The positional concepts of *up* and *down* are relevant to both *art* and *mathematics*.

✓ To include *language arts*, read Nina Crews' *One Hot Summer Day*. This also involves *social studies* because it depicts an African-American girl running, eating, and dancing in the city streets.

What Else I Did

_____

_____

_____

_____

_____

_____

_____

_____

Unit 25
Animals

My Favorite Animal

What It Teaches
- ✓ Familiarity with various animals and their movements
- ✓ Empathy (imagining what it's like to be something else)

What You'll Need
No equipment or materials needed

What to Do
- ✓ Ask the children to tell you about their favorite animals. What do they like best about them? What size are they? How do they move?
- ✓ Choose one favorite at a time, and ask all the children to depict that animal in her or his own way. Continue the process, using all – or as many as possible – of the children's responses.

How to Ensure Success
Different children will have different interpretations of how each animal looks and moves. That's fine – and to be encouraged.

Authenticity isn't necessarily the goal at first. For instance, if a child depicts a cat while moving on two feet, allow it!

What Else You Can Do
- ✓ When the children are ready to work in pairs, have them choose partners. The first partner depicts the actions of an animal of his or her choice (without making any sounds). The second partner must guess and then imitate the animal. The children then reverse roles and continue the process.

More Curriculum Connectors
- ✓ Discussing favorite animals and the reasons for the children's choices incorporates *language* arts into the activity. You also could read books such as *ABC Animals Alphabet in Motion* by Sarina Simon or *Animals Black and White* by Phyllis Limbacher Tildes.
- ✓ The cooperation involved in "What Else You Can Do" qualifies it as *social studies*, as does the fostering of empathy.
- ✓ To involve *music*, you can choose from the many animal-related children's albums available.

What Else I Did

_____

_____

_____

_____

_____

_____

_____

_____

What It Teaches
- ✓ Familiarity with rabbits and kangaroos
- ✓ Size
- ✓ The movement element of force
- ✓ Experience with the locomotor skill of jumping
- ✓ Empathy

What You'll Need
Pictures of rabbits and kangaroos

What to Do
- ✓ Talk to the children about rabbits and kangaroos while showing them pictures of both, if possible. Which is the bigger and which is the smaller? Which would be the heavier of the two? How do these animals move? Which would jump most heavily?
- ✓ Invite the children to move like rabbits and kangaroos, alternating from one to the other.
- ✓ To vary the experience, challenge them to move in straight, curving, and zigzag pathways and at slower and faster speeds. How high can they make their rabbits and kangaroos jump?

How to Ensure Success
Remind the children that rabbits and kangaroos are very *quiet* animals that usually move soundlessly.

At first, allow the children to interpret each animal's movements in his or her own way, even if that means they're not demonstrating size and weight accurately. Later, as you repeat this activity, use follow-up questions to guide them toward discovering the size and weight differences.

What Else You Can Do
- ✓ Use other pairs of animals to similarly explore contrasts. For example, the activity Kitty Cats and Dinosaurs also demonstrates contrasts in size and force of movement. The Tortoise and the Hare is excellent for exploring contrasts in the movement element of time.

More Curriculum Connectors
- ✓ Size, as well as the quantitative concepts of light and heavy, are part of *mathematics*.
- ✓ Empathy is essential to *social studies*.
- ✓ Read *The Tortoise and the Hare* with the children to bring in *language arts*. *Pouch!* by

David Ezra Stein is the story of a young kangaroo.

What Else I Did

_____

_____

_____

_____

_____

_____

_____

_____

Giddy-Up

What It Teaches
- ✓ Familiarity with horses
- ✓ Practice with the locomotor skill of galloping
- ✓ Empathy

What You'll Need
No equipment or materials needed

What to Do
- ✓ Talk to the children about horses. Have they ever ridden one? Have they seen horses in person or on television? What are some colors of horses they've seen? How do horses move? Discuss galloping with the children.
- ✓ Challenge the children to move like horses, encouraging them to pretend they're in an open field, jumping fences, going up and down steep hills, and stopping for occasional drinks of water.

How to Ensure Success
By asking the children to simply pretend to be horses – rather than telling them to gallop – you ensure the children will all experience success. The children who can gallop will likely do so, and those who can't will still be able to do what you've asked.

Some children can learn to gallop through imitation, so if you join in the fun yourself, children can witness the proper way to execute this locomotor skill. Be sure they know you don't require that they do *exactly* as you're doing.

What Else You Can Do
- ✓ Once all the children in your group can gallop, introduce the element of time into the exercise by discussing the difference between a canter and a gallop (cantering is smoother and slower than galloping). Alternately call out the words "gallop" and "canter," to which the children respond accordingly.

More Curriculum Connectors
- ✓ Empathy is a component of *social studies*.
- ✓ Exploring the words "canter" and "gallop" is part of *language arts*. Also, you might share Tony Yelle's *Giddy-Up, Horsey!* It has a multicultural component, which adds another *social studies* lesson.
- ✓ If you accompany this activity with a song that has a galloping rhythm (something in a 2/4 meter is most appropriate), you can incorporate *music*.

What Else I Did

_____
_____
_____
_____
_____
_____
_____
_____

Creepy-Crawly

What It Teaches
- ✓ Experience with cross-lateral movement
- ✓ Experience with a low level in space
- ✓ Empathy

What You'll Need
No equipment or materials needed

What to Do
- ✓ Ask the children to name some of the animals that move along or very near the ground. (Possibilities include snakes, lizards, chameleons, alligators and crocodiles, and seals.)
- ✓ Invite them either to move like their favorite of the animals mentioned or like all of them, one after another, as you call out the name of each.

How to Ensure Success
Authenticity is far less important than the opportunity to experience cross-lateral movement. As long as the children are crawling (moving with the tummy on the floor) and creeping (moving on all fours) allow them to depict each animal according to their own interpretations.

What Else You Can Do
- ✓ The Snake is an activity requiring a great deal of cooperation. Once the children are developmentally ready to handle the responsibility, it's beneficial – and fun. The game begins with partners lying on their stomach, one behind the other. The child in back holds onto the ankles of the child in front, forming a two-person snake. These two-person snakes begin to slither around the room, linking up with each other. The snake continues to grow until all the children are linked, creating one long snake!

More Curriculum Connectors
- ✓ The positional concept of *low* is a component of both *art* and *mathematics*.
- ✓ Empathy is a part of *social studies*, as is the cooperation required in the alternate activity.
- ✓ Read *Snakes* and/or *Alligators and Crocodiles*, by Gail Gibbons.

What Else I Did

_____

_____

_____

Ducks, Cows, Cats, and Dogs

What It Teaches
- ✓ Awareness of various animals and their sounds
- ✓ Experience with cross-lateral movement
- ✓ Sound discrimination
- ✓ Cooperation
- ✓ Empathy

What You'll Need
No equipment or materials needed

What to Do
- ✓ Talk to the children about each of the animals named in the title of this game adapted from Docheff.[17] What sound does each of them make?
- ✓ Explain the rules of the game to the children:
  - Ask the children to space themselves throughout the room. Whisper the name of one of these animals in each player's ear.
  - Once each child has been assigned an animal, have the children all close their eyes and get on their hands and knees.
  - At your start signal, the "animals" begin to move, making the appropriate sounds. The object of the game is for like animals to find one another. When they've done so, they stop making their sounds and sit and watch the others who are still trying.

How to Ensure Success
For the youngest children, choose to play with only two or three of the animals cited in the activity title.

Help the children by letting them know when all the dogs, for example, have found each other. Once they realize they've successfully reached their goal, they can be an audience to the children still playing.

What Else You Can Do
- ✓ To make this activity more challenging for older children, use all four of the animals (ducks, cows, cats, and dogs). If the group is large enough, add other animals with familiar sounds, like pigs, chickens, or sheep.

---

[17] Docheff, D.M. (1992). *Hey, let's play! A collection of P.E. games and activities for the classroom teacher*. Elmo WA: Dodge R Productions.

More Curriculum Connectors

✓ Because this is a listening – or sound discrimination – activity, it involves both *music* and *language arts*.

✓ Empathy and cooperation qualify the game as *social studies*.

✓ Once all the "animals" have found each other, ask the children to count the number in each group, making it a *mathematics* experience.

✓ To incorporate *art*, ask the children to draw their assigned animals.

Unit 26

Simple Science

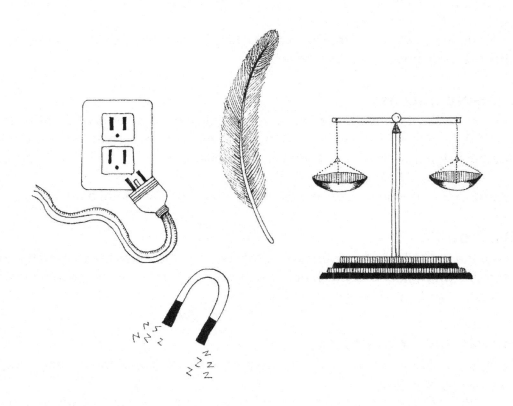

What It Teaches
- ✓ An introduction to flotation
- ✓ The movement element of force
- ✓ The concepts of up and down

What You'll Need
Chiffon scarves (one per child) or a substitute – paper towel squares, feathers, bubbles, or something else that will demonstrate the concept

What to Do
- ✓ Demonstrate for the children how bubbles, feathers, or chiffon scarves float through the air. Is the movement light or heavy? What words would they use to describe the movement?
- ✓ If you have scarves available for the children, hand them out and let each child explore for him- or herself how the scarves gently float back down to the floor or ground – no matter how hard they may toss them up.
- ✓ Challenge the children to pretend to be floating in the air. Is the movement strong or light? Are their muscles tight or loose?

How to Ensure Success
Ask questions about the movement's force, using words such as *gentle* and *easy*, to help get the right idea across. Having the visual example of scarves, feathers, or bubbles will contribute significantly to the children's comprehension.

Pretend to be a gentle breeze keeping the "scarves" (the children) adrift.

What Else You Can Do
- ✓ Encourage the children to experiment with a variety of items at the water table to determine which float and which don't. They can then simulate the movement of both the floating and the sinking items.

More Curriculum Connectors
- ✓ Asking the children to find words to describe the movement of the floating item(s) involves *language arts*.
- ✓ The positional concepts of up and down fall under the headings of both *art* and *mathematics*.

What Else I Did

_____

_____

_____

_____

_____

_____

_____

_____

What It Teaches
✓ An introduction to gravity
✓ The concepts of up and down

What You'll Need
Beanbags (one per child)

What to Do
✓ Talk to the children in simple terms about why things don't stay up in the air when you toss them there. If you'd prefer not to use the word *gravity* yet, tell them the "pull of the earth" brings the objects back down.
✓ Hand out the beanbags and instruct the children to toss them gently toward the ceiling, watching as they come back down to the floor.
✓ Challenge the children to each count how many seconds it takes for their beanbags to come back down (or how high they can count before the beanbag reaches the floor).
✓ To make the activity more challenging, ask them to see how many times they can clap or turn around before the beanbag reaches the floor. If the children wish to try to catch their beanbags instead of letting them drop, encourage them to do so; they'll need all the practice they can get in eye-hand coordination.

How to Ensure Success
If you don't have a very large space for this activity, and you can't do it outside, instruct the children not to toss their beanbags high – because that's the only way to ensure that the beanbags land somewhere near the children tossing them!

What Else You Can Do
✓ Explain to the children that, just like objects, people can't stay up in the air either. Challenge them to see how high they can jump, hop, or leap into the air – and to see if they can stay up there! (They'll be trying with all their might, so be sure they land with their knees bent and their heels coming all the way down to the floor – to save wear and tear on their knees and shins.)
✓ Invite the children to toss objects of varying sizes and weights into the air. Do the size and weight make any difference in how fast the objects fall?

More Curriculum Connectors
✓ The positional concepts of up and down are important to both *mathematics* and *art*. Counting, size, and weight are also mathematics concepts.
✓ *Floating in Space*, by Franklin M. Branley, is about how astronauts move and cope with

weightlessness in space. This would add a *language arts* component, while discussion of the occupation of astronauts ties in to *social studies*.

✓ Rae Pica and Richard Gardzina's CD *Wiggle, Giggle, & Shake* includes a song called "The Astronaut." It gives children the opportunity to pretend to move weightlessly – without the effects of gravity – and brings in *music*.

What Else I Did

_____
_____
_____
_____
_____
_____
_____
_____
_____

It's Electric!

What It Teaches
- ✓ An introduction to the conduction of electricity
- ✓ **Sequential movement**[18]
- ✓ Cooperation

What You'll Need
No equipment or materials needed

What to Do
- ✓ Ask the children for examples of things that run on electricity. Then explain that when one of those things is plugged into the wall, the electricity is "conducted" (it travels) through the plug and the cord and into the object.
- ✓ Ask the children to form a standing circle with you, and to hold hands. Squeeze the hand of one of the children next to you, and ask him or her to squeeze the hand of the next child, and so on, all the way around the circle. Explain that, like electricity, the squeeze is traveling (being conducted) all around the circle, as though they were an electrical cord.
- ✓ Try it again, this time adding a vibration to your body as you squeeze so they can really envision the "electricity" flowing.

How to Ensure Success
Having you as part of the circle will definitely help, but if the children express any confusion over the idea of sequential movement, instruct one child at a time to squeeze the hand of the next child, while you call them by name.

What Else You Can Do
- ✓ Remind the children of some of the things they said that electricity is necessary to operate. Invite them to choose one item and to demonstrate how it looks, moves, or functions.

More Curriculum Connectors
- ✓ Sequential is a *mathematics* concept.
- ✓ The cooperation required enhances *social studies*.
- ✓ Among many books written about electricity are *Oscar and the Bird* by Geoff Waring and *Charged Up: The Story of Electricity* by Jacqui Bailey. These involve the children in *language arts*.

---

[18] **sequential movement** Movements done in sequence, such as the "wave" by fans at a sporting event.

What Else I Did

Balancing Act

What It Teaches
- ✓ Balance
- ✓ Identification of center of gravity
- ✓ Body-part identification
- ✓ Counting

What You'll Need
Mat or carpeting would be preferable to the bare floor

What to Do
- ✓ Challenge the children to balance on body parts that you designate while you count to five. Have them try to remain as still as they can while you're counting. You might include parts such as hands and feet, hands and knees, knees and elbows, feet and bottom, or hands and bottom. More challenging would be one hand and one foot, and just bottom, knees, or feet on tiptoe.
- ✓ For the next step (now or at a later time), challenge the children to balance on a certain *number* of parts on the floor, again holding as still as possible for a count of five. (You'll be able to assess immediately which children are having difficulty counting.)

How to Ensure Success
If necessary, count aloud to five yourself, at first counting quickly, then gradually lengthening the amount of time it takes to get from one to five.

When working with numbers of body parts, begin with a higher number, such as five, and work your way down to one (if that's feasible for your group). Be sure to ask for multiple solutions to each challenge. Encourage the children to each find at least two different ways to balance on, for example, four body parts.

Keep in mind that children don't necessarily think as we do. For them, a foot sometimes counts as one body part and sometimes as five parts. Sometimes a bottom counts as one body part and sometimes as two!

What Else You Can Do
- ✓ Once the children are ready, explore the more difficult concept of balance and recovery with them. Ask them to balance on their knees or their bottom only and lean in different directions, going as far as they can without tipping over, and then return to their original positions.
- ✓ More challenging is the concept of counterbalance, in which partners create balances that couldn't be possible for just one person (for example, leaning against each other,

back to back).

More Curriculum Connectors

✓ Counting, whether it be the number of seconds a position is held or the number of body parts, means these activities are related to *mathematics*.

✓ The alternative activity focusing on counterbalance requires cooperation between partners, which links it to *social studies*.

✓ To incorporate *music*, play "High Wire Artist," from Hap Palmer's *Easy Does It*.

What Else I Did

_____

_____

_____

_____

_____

_____

_____

_____

The Machine

What It Teaches
- ✓ Awareness of the contribution that parts make to machinery as a whole
- ✓ Cooperation
- ✓ Practice with nonlocomotor movement

What You'll Need
No equipment or materials needed

What to Do
- ✓ Have one child begin by repeatedly performing a movement that can be executed in one spot. Then have a second child stand near the first and contribute a second movement that relates in some way to the first. (For example, if the first child is performing an up-down motion by bending and stretching, the second child might choose to do the reverse, standing beside her or his classmate.)
- ✓ Add a third child, who is to perform a movement of his or her own. (To continue with the preceding example, the third child might choose an arm or leg motion timed to move between the two bodies that are bending and stretching.)
- ✓ Ask the first three children to continue their movements as each remaining child adds a functioning "part" to the machine.
- ✓ Once all the parts are functioning, ask the children to each make a sound that corresponds to her or his movement.

How to Ensure Success
At first, you may have to suggest movement possibilities to the children.

Remind the children that they may choose any movements as long as they don't interfere with the actions of others and that they contribute in some way to the "machine."

What Else You Can Do
- ✓ The six simple machines are the lever, wheel, pulley, inclined plane, screw, and wedge. Bring attention to some of these by asking the children to roll like wheels and twist like screwdrivers (or screws being driven in) and to demonstrate the shapes of inclines and wedges with their body or body parts. Levers with which the children are familiar – and which they can imitate – include scissors, wheelbarrows, and seesaws.

More Curriculum Connectors
- ✓ The cooperation required of the principal activity is a component of *social studies*.

- ✓ The production of sound, as required in the final step of the main activity, falls under the heading of *music*.
- ✓ To include *language arts*, read David Macaulay's *The Way Things Work* or Gillian Gosman's *Wheels and Axles in Action*.

What Else I Did

_____

_____

_____

_____

_____

_____

_____

_____

What It Teaches
- ✓ Principles of magnetics
- ✓ Cooperation
- ✓ **Directionality**[19]

What You'll Need
A set of magnets

What to Do
- ✓ Demonstrate for the children how opposite poles attract (stick together) and identical poles repel (move away from each other). Explain that one end is called a "north" pole and the other a "south" pole.
- ✓ Magically turn the children themselves into magnets: Ask them to move around the room as though they were magnets with only north or south poles. What happens when two such magnets (children) approach each other?

How to Ensure Success
If the idea of north and south poles is too complicated for the group, use terms such as "one end" and the "other end," or anything else you deem appropriate.

Remind the children, for safety reasons, that repelling magnets never touch one another.

What Else You Can Do
- ✓ Assign half of the class to act as north poles and the other half as south poles (or ask them to decide themselves which they would like to be). The north poles point a finger or hand toward the ceiling, while the south poles point toward the floor. Now what happens when two magnets get close to each other? (If two identical poles meet, they repel; if two opposite poles meet, they stick together.)

More Curriculum Connectors
- ✓ Cooperation is key to *social studies*.
- ✓ Directionality is a component of both *art* and *mathematics*.
- ✓ "Magical Magnets" is one of the songs on Hap Palmer's *Can Cockatoos Count by Twos?* This will incorporate *music*.
- ✓ To involve *language arts*, read *Magnet Max* by Monica Lozano Hughes, or Natalie Rosinsky's *Magnets: Pulling Together, Pushing Apart*.

---

[19] **directionality** An awareness of direction (right, left, up, down, forward, backward, etc.)

What Else I Did

_____
_____
_____
_____
_____
_____
_____
_____
_____

Section Six

Social Studies

Lessons in social studies for young children begin with the children themselves – because that's where their world begins. Self-concept, therefore, is the logical starting point in the early childhood social studies curriculum. The child's world then extends, respectively, to family, friends, neighborhood, and the community in general.

As children learn about themselves and about each other, they discover how they are alike and different. They explore feelings, rules for living (particularly with regard to safety), holidays and celebrations, traditions and cultures, and the jobs that keep a community functioning. The following games and activities explore topics that typically come under the heading of social studies in early childhood settings: self-concept, families and friends, holidays and celebrations, occupations, and transportation.

Because being a friend or family member involves being and working together, Unit 28 consists primarily of cooperative games. Unit 29, devoted to holidays and celebrations, includes activities of a generic nature, focusing on the spirit of holidays and celebrations rather than specific occasions. (Possibilities abound for exploring specific holidays through movement, as each offers a multitude of images. Children can move like black cats and ghosts at Halloween; Santa, elves, and reindeer at Christmas; cooks at Thanksgiving; and so on.)

Under occupations, unit 30, I've chosen to give children a sense of the many opportunities they have available to them in the future, regardless of gender. I've included an activity related to performing and visual arts so as not to exclude less traditional choices.

Unit 27
Self-Concept

"If You're Happy"

What It Teaches

✓ Awareness and expression of emotions

What You'll Need

No equipment or materials needed

What to Do

✓ Teach the children the first verse of "If You're Happy," performing it the traditional way. The lyrics are as follows:

If you're happy and you know it, clap your hands.
If you're happy and you know it, clap your hands.
If you're happy and you know it, then your face will surely show it.
If you're happy and you know it, clap your hands.

✓ Ask the children for suggestions of other movements to demonstrate happiness (tapping feet, waving hello, nodding the head, shouting "hooray," etc.).
✓ Perform the song repeatedly, using as many of the children's suggestions as time allows.

How to Ensure Success

Ask the children to tell you about times they've been really happy. How did their faces look at the time? What movements did their hands and/or body perform when they felt that way?

What Else You Can Do

✓ Ask the children for suggestions of other emotions they could sing about. Possibilities include feeling sad, tired, angry, or hungry. What motions and facial expressions go along with the feelings they choose? How would they sing the song if they were feeling that way? Perform the song, using as many of their suggestions as time allows.

More Curriculum Connectors

✓ Singing is one of the five ways in which children experience *music*.
✓ Learning and creating song lyrics are part of *language arts*, as is discussing feelings of happiness and their causes.

What Else I Did

_____
_____
_____
_____
_____
_____
_____
_____

Oh, What a Feeling

What It Teaches
✓ Awareness and expression of emotions

What You'll Need
No equipment or materials needed

What to Do
✓ Ask the children to demonstrate how their face would look if they were feeling sad, mad, tired, proud, scared, and happy. How would their whole body look?
✓ Challenge them to show you how they would walk if they were feeling those same emotions.

How to Ensure Success
Talk to the children about these different emotions and times when they may have experienced them. What makes them sad, mad, etc.?

What Else You Can Do
✓ Ask the children to demonstrate these same emotions with just their face, just their hands, or both together.

More Curriculum Connectors
✓ Asking the children to describe events that caused them to feel certain emotions constitutes *language arts*. Possible books include *Lots of Feelings* by Shelley Rotner, *The Way I Feel* by Janan Cain, and Aliki's *Feelings*.
✓ Sing selections from Hap Palmer's *Ideas, Thoughts, and Feelings* brings in *music*, as does "The Way I Feel" from Rae Pica and Richard Gardzina's *Wiggle, Giggle, and Shake*.

What Else I Did

_____
_____
_____
_____
_____
_____
_____

"Punchinello"

What It Teaches
- ✓ Self-awareness
- ✓ Self-confidence

What You'll Need
No equipment or materials needed

What to Do
- ✓ Ask the children to form a circle, with one child in the center ("Punchinello").
- ✓ Have the children in the circle chant, "What can you do, Punchinello, funny fellow? What can you do, Punchinello, funny you?"
- ✓ Invite the child in the center to choose a skill, movement or shape to demonstrate.
- ✓ The rest of the children now chant, "We can do it, too, Punchinello, funny fellow. We can do it, too, Punchinello, funny you" – and they do!

How to Ensure Success
If you have children who are too shy at first to be in the center, ask only those children who want to demonstrate to act as Punchinello.

Be sure the children realize that everyone who wants a turn will get a turn. (Be sure you leave enough time to keep that promise.)

Explain that Punchinello can demonstrate any skill, movement, or shape that he or she wants to demonstrate, but that it should be something everybody else will be able to do too.

What Else You Can Do
- ✓ Play Pass a Face, in which the children sit in a circle and one child begins by making a face that is "passed" to the child to his or her right or left. That child makes the *same* face and passes it along in the same direction. When the face has been passed all around the circle, the process is repeated, with a different child beginning.
- ✓ Play Pass a Movement, in which the children form a standing circle and pass around an *action*. The first child might, for instance, bend at the waist and straighten. Each child, in succession, must do the same.

More Curriculum Connectors
- ✓ The rhyme in the original game is a *language arts* concept, as is the chanting of "Punchinello."

- ✓ The sequential movement of the alternative games incorporates *mathematics*.
- ✓ Being able to physically replicate what the eyes see is an essential quality of *art*.

What Else I Did

_____
_____
_____
_____
_____
_____
_____
_____
_____

Unit 28
Families and Friends

What It Teaches
- ✓ Awareness and appreciation of others
- ✓ Sequential movement
- ✓ An introduction to laterality

What You'll Need
No equipment or materials needed

What to Do
- ✓ Have the children stand in a circle holding hands. Ask one child to raise the arm of the child to her right or left, saying, "This is my friend...." The child whose arm has been raised is to announce his name and then raise the arm of the next child in the circle, saying, "This is my friend...."
- ✓ Continue the process all the way around the circle, with the arms remaining raised until the last child has had a chance to say her name. When that happens, have the children take a deep bow for a job well done.

How to Ensure Success
Until the children are familiar with this game, stand in the circle with them and start the activity yourself.

If necessary, help the children with reminders of who's next, to keep arms in the air, etc.

What Else You Can Do
- ✓ This game, adapted from Orlick[20], is a wonderful way for children to learn one another's names. Once they have learned them, they can introduce each other: One child raises the arm of the child to his right or left and says, "This is my friend [Tori]."
- ✓ Play a game called Who's Missing? to create more awareness among the children. In this game the children sit with their eyes closed. Tap one child on the shoulder, and have her quietly sneak away to a predetermined spot out of sight of the other children. When you tell the children it's okay to open their eyes, they must look around and figure out which one of them is missing!

More Curriculum Connectors
- ✓ Lifting the arms high and moving sequentially around the circle qualifies This Is My Friend as an exercise in *mathematics*.

---

[20] Orlick, T. (2006). *Cooperative games and sports: Joyful activities for everyone.* Champaign IL: Human Kinetics.

✓ The alternate activity relies on observational skills, which are essential to *science*.
✓ The concept of friendship is explored in books such as James Marshall's *George and Martha One Fine Day*, Miriam Cohen's *Best Friends*, Taro Goni's *My Friends*, Helme Heine's *Friends*, and Kristen DeBear's *Be Quiet, Marina*. You can use these books to add *language arts*.

What Else I Did

_____
_____
_____
_____
_____
_____
_____
_____
_____

What It Teaches
- ✓ Awareness of family roles
- ✓ Role-playing/self-expression

What You'll Need
No equipment or materials needed

What to Do
- ✓ Talk to the children about their families, asking how many members their families include, whether they're the oldest or youngest sibling or an only child, etc. This will give the children a chance to contemplate their families and how they may be alike or different from their classmates' families.
- ✓ Discuss the various roles that different family members play in the household. For instance, the children themselves may be responsible for certain chores around the house. What are their siblings' responsibilities? Maybe Dad cooks and Mom loads the dishwasher. Does Grandma fish or knit? Does Grandpa garden or ski?
- ✓ Have the children, one at a time, demonstrate – through movement alone – a role played or task accomplished by either themselves or one of their family members. After a child has demonstrated, ask the rest of the children to guess what the task or role was and then to perform the movement(s) themselves.
- ✓ Repeat until every child has a chance to demonstrate.

How to Ensure Success
If you have too large a group or if the children aren't ready to handle this challenge all at once, repeat the process once or twice. Be sure the children realize they'll all have a turn eventually.

If the children aren't forthcoming with responses of their own, prompt them with questions such as: "Who does the dishes?" "Do you have a pet?" "Whose job is it to feed the pet?"

What Else You Can Do
- ✓ Talk to the children about some of the activities the adults in the family perform that they'll one day learn to do too. Using their responses, ask them to depict some of these activities. Possibilities include driving a car, grocery shopping, or playing a sport such as tennis or golf.

More Curriculum Connectors

✓ The discussion of family roles is a facet of *language arts*. You might also read Mercer Mayer's book *Me Too!* or Todd Parr's *The Family Book*, which celebrates families and all the varieties they come in.

✓ Incorporate music with selections from Thomas Moore's album *The Family*.

What Else I Did

_____

_____

_____

_____

_____

_____

_____

_____

Palm to Palm

What It Teaches
- ✓ Cooperation
- ✓ The movement element of shape

What You'll Need
No equipment or materials needed

What to Do
- ✓ Have the children choose partners and stand facing each other, close enough to touch.
- ✓ Have the first child assume a shape with her or his arms, with palms facing those of the partner (for example, the first child raises both arms above the head with palms facing the second child). The partner then forms the identical shape, touching palms with those of the first child.
- ✓ As soon as contact is made, have the first child choose a new arm position, and continue the activity accordingly.
- ✓ After a while, have the partners reverse roles.

How to Ensure Success
Before beginning, have the children experiment with the different shapes they can make with their arms.

Once the game begins, indicate that any shape is acceptable as long as palms face the partner. If the children are unclear on this concept, physically assist them.

What Else You Can Do
- ✓ When the children show you that they can successfully match palms, have them try Footsie Rolls! In this game, pairs of children lie on their back with the soles of their feet together and then attempt to roll without their feet breaking contact. (Successful experiences with log rolls is a prerequisite.) Even if they don't get very far, children find this game hilarious.

More Curriculum Connectors
- ✓ The element of shape is vital to both *art* and *mathematics*.
- ✓ To further promote the idea of cooperation and include *language arts*, read Nicholas Oldland's *Walk on the Wild Side*, which promotes teamwork.

What Else I Did

_____
_____
_____
_____
_____
_____
_____
_____

Musical Hoops

What It Teaches
- ✓ Cooperation
- ✓ Practice with locomotor skills
- ✓ Problem solving

What You'll Need
One hoop per child

Any lively recording

What to Do
- ✓ Scatter hoops throughout the room and instruct the children to each stand inside one.
- ✓ Start playing the musical selection you've chosen, and have the children begin to walk around the room. As the children are walking, remove one of the hoops.
- ✓ When the music stops, ask the children to step inside the closest hoop, sharing the ones remaining.
- ✓ Assign the children a different locomotor skill for the next round, and begin the music again, once more removing a hoop.
- ✓ Continue the game until just one hoop remains, which the children must decide how to share.

How to Ensure Success
If the children are familiar with the traditional version of Musical Chairs, reassure them that no one is left out of this game.

Give the children a chance to solve problems on their own. If they can't figure out a way to share the dwindling number of hoops, make suggestions. One possibility is for each child to place just one foot (or one toe!) inside a hoop.

Suggest only those locomotor skills you're sure everyone in the group can perform.

What Else You Can Do
- ✓ Substitute chairs for the hoops, playing a game of Cooperative Musical Chairs. This is more challenging than Musical Hoops.

More Curriculum Connectors
- ✓ *Music* is an important part of this activity.
- ✓ The listening skills required – differentiating between sound and silence – fall under the

230

heading of both *music* and *language arts*. Read Lauren Murphy Payne's *We Can Get Along* to reinforce the concept of cooperative behavior.

What Else I Did

_____
_____
_____
_____
_____
_____
_____
_____

It Takes Two

What It Teaches
- ✓ Cooperation
- ✓ Problem solving
- ✓ Body-part identification

What You'll Need
No equipment or materials needed

What to Do
- ✓ Ask the children to choose partners.
- ✓ After the children select partners, ask them to connect various body parts – one at a time – and see how many ways they can move without breaking the connection. Possible connections include right or left hands, right or left elbows, one or both knees, right or left feet, or backs.

How to Ensure Success
Remind the children they have two challenges: to stay connected and to discover how many ways they can move while connected.

If necessary, make suggestions for different locomotor skills, changes in level, changes in direction, etc. Be sure to call out all the different responses you see. This is validating for the children and provides new ideas for them.

Be sure to give the children ample time to explore all the possibilities with one connection before moving on to the next.

What Else You Can Do
- ✓ For more of a challenge, connect *nonmatching* body parts (for example, a hand to an elbow, an elbow to a shoulder, or a hand to a back).
- ✓ Play a game of Synchronized Partners, which requires pairs of children to cooperate *without* touching. In this game, one partner begins by repeatedly performing a movement that can be executed in one spot. His or her partner stands near the first and performs a movement that relates in some way – without interfering – to the first. After they've had a chance to experience the "synchronicity," the partners reverse roles and try again with new movements.

More Curriculum Connectors
- ✓ Matching and nonmatching (body parts) are *mathematics* concepts.

- ✓ Body-part identification qualifies as *science* for young children.
- ✓ Read *Share and Take Turns* by Cheri J. Meiners, to incorporate *language arts*.

What Else I Did

_____
_____
_____
_____
_____
_____
_____
_____
_____

Unit 29
Holidays and Celebrations

Pass the Present

What It Teaches
- ✓ Cooperation
- ✓ Sharing
- ✓ The spirit of holidays and celebrations

What You'll Need
No equipment or materials needed

What to Do
- ✓ Talk to the children about the spirit of giving and sharing, which is what holidays and celebrations are all about.
- ✓ With the children sitting in a circle, choose one child to begin. Have that child stand and depict the movement or shape of a favorite present (or one she would like to receive).
- ✓ Have the child to her right or left (depending on which direction you've chosen to move) imitate that movement or shape and then choose a movement of his own. Continue around the circle until every child has a chance to "pass a present."
- ✓ End the game with the first child imitating the shape or movement of the last child.

How to Ensure Success
For maximum involvement from the children waiting their turn, ask them to guess what each present is.

What Else You Can Do
- ✓ Play the game in a manner similar to "Punchinello." The child whose turn it is moves to the center of the circle, then *all* the children imitate his or her movement or shape before the next child takes a turn. (This may be preferable if you have a very large group, as it eliminates the waiting.)

More Curriculum Connectors
- ✓ Shape is a component of both *art* and *mathematics*.
- ✓ Holiday *music* adds another dimension.
- ✓ To further incorporate *art*, before or after the game, ask the children to draw their favorite present.
- ✓ To include both *art* and *language arts*, share *The Quiltmaker's Gift* with the children. Written by Jeff Brumbeau and illustrated by Gail DeMarchen, it's the story of an unhappy king who things acquiring "things" would bring him joy.

What Else I Did

_____

_____

_____

_____

_____

_____

_____

_____

Light the Candles

What It Teaches
- ✓ Awareness of symbolism representing the holiday spirit
- ✓ Experience with the movement elements of shape, time, force, and flow

What You'll Need
Candles and matches (optional)

What to Do
- ✓ Talk to the children about the various times candles are used to help celebrate a holiday or special occasion. (Possibilities include birthday, Hanukkah, and Halloween.)
- ✓ If you have a candle available, show it to the children, talking about its shape and size and what it's made of. Is it hard or soft? Light the candle and ask the children to concentrate on the movement of the flame. What words would they use to describe it? Is it gentle or strong? If you have the time, take a few minutes to watch the candle begin to melt, and discuss this process as well. Then suddenly blow it out. (You can hold this discussion without a candle; simply ask the children to recall one they've seen.)
- ✓ Ask the children to each pretend to *be* a candle, at first made of hard wax and unlit.
- ✓ Then pretend to light the candles. How would they demonstrate the flame flickering on top?
- ✓ Invite them to show you how they slowly melt. After they've had a few moments to demonstrate, suddenly "blow them out." How would they show you they've been "extinguished?"

How to Ensure Success
The more words you and the children use to describe the candle and the process, the more accurately they'll be able to demonstrate. If necessary, repeat some of the words while you lead the activity.

What Else You Can Do
- ✓ Ask the children to make a fist (or both fists), pretending their fingers are candles about to be lit. While counting aloud with you, have them "light" (open) one finger at a time. When they've reached the predetermined number (for example, the number representing their age or the number 8 for the eight nights of Hanukkah), have them "extinguish" (close) one finger at a time. Once they can demonstrate this, each time you repeat the process, increase the tempo at which you call out the numbers.

More Curriculum Connectors
- ✓ The concept of shape is related to both *art* and *mathematics* (the latter of which is also

explored in "What Else You Can Do").

✓ The concepts of fire and melting fall under the heading of *science*, as does the movement element of force.

✓ The discussion of candles is part of *language arts*. Among the books related to Hanukkah are *Hershel and the Hanukkah Goblins* by Trina Schart Hyman, and *Maccabee Jamboree: A Hanukkah Countdown* by Cheri Holland.

✓ Excellent possibilities for incorporating *music* include Steve and Greg's *Holidays and Special Times* and Hap Palmer's *Holiday Songs and Rhythms* and *Holiday Magic*.

What Else I Did

_____

_____

_____

_____

_____

_____

_____

_____

Let's Hear It for the USA

What It Teaches
- ✓ Awareness of patriotism and its symbols
- ✓ The movement element of shape

What You'll Need
A United States flag or a picture of one (optional)

What to Do
- ✓ Talk to the children about holidays celebrating various aspects of our country (e.g., Independence Day, Memorial Day, Presidents' Day, and Flag Day). Discuss the United States flag, which represents our country. Talk to them about the number of stars and stripes and the proper way to treat the flag.
- ✓ Ask the children to demonstrate a flag being raised up a flagpole, waving proudly in the breeze, being lowered, and being folded.
- ✓ Challenge them to show you the shape of first the stripes, and then the stars.

How to Ensure Success
Encourage the children in their depictions by verbally describing each step of the process. For instance, does the flag move slowly or quickly up the flagpole? Does it move smoothly or jerkily?

If the children have a chance to watch a flag being raised at school or at a public building (or a video of this event), it will have more meaning for them.

What Else You Can Do
- ✓ In the spirit of celebrating patriotism, ask the children to show you fireworks, perhaps to the accompaniment of Tchaikovsky's *1812 Overture*.
- ✓ Hold a "parade" in the classroom or on the playground. Who and what are the various participants in a parade? Which do the children want to be? If they'd like to be in the marching band, what instruments do they want to play? (Accompany this activity with a John Philip Sousa march or selections from Hap Palmer's *Marching*.)

More Curriculum Connectors
- ✓ The element of shape is related to both *art* and *mathematics*. The latter can be explored further by counting stars and stripes.
- ✓ Accompanying the "What Else You Can do" activities with the suggested compositions incorporates *music*. You might accompany the main activity with a patriotic song too.
- ✓ *Language arts* and multicultural education (*social studies*) can be part of the experience

239

by reading *Who Belongs Here? An American Story* by Margy Burns Knight, a book about immigration in our country (also available in Spanish).

What Else I Did

_____

_____

_____

_____

_____

_____

_____

_____

Unit 30
Occupations

"This Is the Way We..."

What It Teaches
✓ Awareness of and respect for various occupations and career choices

What You'll Need
No equipment or materials needed

What to Do
✓ Talk to the children about the different jobs it takes to run a community. Ask all the children, in turn, what they want to be when they grow up.
✓ As each child answers your question, ask him or her to demonstrate an action performed by a person holding that job. Then have the rest of the children imitate the action.
✓ Repeat the process until every child has a turn.

How to Ensure Success
If a child can't think of an appropriate action to go along with the chosen occupation, suggest several possibilities, and allow the child to choose which one to perform.

What Else You Can Do
✓ Call out an occupation and challenge the children to call out a corresponding action. Choose one at a time for the children to perform while singing, "This is the way we..." to the tune of "The Mulberry Bush" (for example, "This is the way we paint the house" or "This is the way we slide down the pole").

More Curriculum Connectors
✓ The discussion of various occupations brings *language arts* into the activity. You also might read *Helpers in My Community* by Bobbie Kalman.
✓ The piggyback song suggested in "What Else You Can Do" involves both *language arts* and *music*.

What Else I Did

_____

_____

_____

_____

_____

_____

_____

_____

Equal Opportunity

What It Teaches
- ✓ The concept of options for all, regardless of gender
- ✓ Appreciation for a variety of occupations
- ✓ Role-playing

What You'll Need
No equipment or materials needed

What to Do
- ✓ Talk to the children about various occupations that are frequently associated with one gender or the other, *without* mentioning gender (e.g., chefs, homemakers, hair stylists, police officers, carpenters, dancers). Ask them to tell you some of the tasks that people in these occupations do.
- ✓ Invite the children to act out some of these tasks, one at a time.

How to Ensure Success
For some occupations, you might ask the children to show you specific actions (e.g., a homemaker *washing windows*, or a police officer *directing traffic*) to narrow the possibilities and avoid confusion or, as in the case of the police officer, to eliminate unwanted responses. Otherwise, simply ask them to show you, for instance, a chef or hair stylist *at work*.

To achieve the lesson's objective, encourage *all* the children, regardless of gender, to act out each occupation.

What Else You Can Do
- ✓ Once the children have ample experience with this activity, play a game in which you call out the occupations faster and faster, in random order.
- ✓ Play a game in which the children, one at a time, depict an action related to an occupation of their choosing, with the rest of the children trying to guess the profession.

More Curriculum Connectors
- ✓ Discussion of the various roles performed by people in various occupations constitutes *language arts*. Dee Ready's *Community Helpers* series includes 10 books for kindergarten to grade three focusing on the helping aspects of men and women in common careers.

244

What Else I Did

Makin' Music

What It Teaches
- ✓ Appreciation for an arts-related occupation
- ✓ Role-playing

What You'll Need
Child-sized instruments (optional)

What to Do
- ✓ Talk to the children about rock and roll bands. What instruments are typically found in them?
- ✓ Invite the children to pretend to be in a band, playing the instruments they would like to play.
- ✓ Challenge them to "play" each of the other instruments.

How to Ensure Success
Children generally think first of electric guitars and drums. Be sure to ask them about other possibilities such as keyboards, saxophone, and trumpet. Encourage them to consider the difference between playing an *acoustic* guitar and an electric guitar.

When the children first take part in this activity, they probably will respond by mimicking actions they've seen on television or performed by an older sibling (for example, wildly playing "air guitar"). Once they've had a chance to express themselves, gently encourage them to use as much realism in their depictions as possible. For instance, drummers play several different drums, as well as cymbals. Keyboardists often have two or three keyboards, side by side, or one above another on racks in front of them.

What Else You Can Do
- ✓ Repeat the activity with musical organizations such as orchestras and marching bands, which offer other choices of instruments. If you have child-sized instruments available, hold an actual "parade" in your classroom or around the playground.
- ✓ At various times, when the children are involved in painting, expose them to music performed by different kinds of musical groups. You'll find, for example, that soft orchestral music results in long, flowing strokes of the paintbrush and rock and roll produces short, staccato jabs.
- ✓ Talk to the children about various kinds of *dancers* (ballet, tap, ballroom, hip-hop, etc.), and challenge them to depict the actions of each.

More Curriculum Connectors

✓ This lesson plan develops an appreciation for *music*. You also might use Frank Leto's album, *Rhythm Band Jam*, to introduce rhythm band instruments to the children.

✓ Discussion of the various kinds of musical groups and dancers is a part of *language arts*. To introduce the children to jazz, read Matthew Gollub's *The Jazz Fly*.

✓ Playing music as the children are painting combines *music* and *art*.

What Else I Did

_____

_____

_____

_____

_____

_____

_____

_____

_____

What It Teaches
- ✓ Appreciation for an occupation that often is undervalued
- ✓ Role-playing

What You'll Need
No equipment or materials needed

What to Do
- ✓ Discuss with the children some of the chores involved in keeping house. How many are they responsible for? Which ones?
- ✓ One at a time, call out various housekeeping tasks, and ask the children to show you what it looks like to perform them.

How to Ensure Success
Don't worry about realism at first. Let the children pretend to their hearts' content.

Point out the differences you see in their responses. For example, some children pretend to wash windows horizontally, others vertically, and still others diagonally; some pretend to use a squeegee. Let them know it's all right to find their own way.

What Else You Can Do
- ✓ Ask the children to pretend to be housecleaning objects – for example, a vacuum cleaner, broom, feather duster, dishcloth, sponge, or dishwasher.

More Curriculum Connectors
- ✓ To incorporate *music*, accompany these activities with the children's favorite cleanup song. Or play "It's Clean up Time" from Mr. Al's *Sing Me Some Sanity*.
- ✓ Pretending to be a vacuum cleaner or dishwasher explores the concept of machinery, which falls under the heading of *science*.

What Else I Did

_____
_____
_____
_____
_____
_____
_____
_____

Unit 31
Transportation

"Row, Row, Row Your Boat"

What It Teaches
- ✓ Awareness of certain types of transportation

What You'll Need
Carpet squares (optional)

What to Do
- ✓ If the children don't know the song, teach them to sing "Row, Row, Row Your Boat." If they do know it, review it. The lyrics are:

  Row, row, row your boat
  Gently down the stream
  Merrily, merrily, merrily, merrily
  Life is but a dream.

- ✓ Designate one spot in the room as the starting point and another, as far away as possible, as the finishing point.
- ✓ Ask the children to imagine that the room, or playground, is a big lake and that they're going to row a boat across it. Do they know the motion involved in rowing?
- ✓ At your signal, have the children begin to row, singing, "Row, Row, Row Your Boat."
- ✓ Repeat the activity back and forth across the "lake," as long as the children remain interested.

How to Ensure Success
To offer the children variety and broaden the scope of the activity, suggest different tempos (slow, medium, and fast), pathways (straight, curving, and zigzagging), and amounts of effort (rowing lightly versus rowing strongly).

What Else You Can Do
- ✓ If you have carpet squares available, have each child sit on one and use his or her feet to "scoot" across the lake, still making a rowing action with the arms. (This is great exercise!)
- ✓ Repeat the main activity with other modes of transportation, creating the appropriate piggyback lyrics (for example, "Paddle, paddle, paddle the canoe...").
- ✓ Sing and act out "The Wheels on the Bus." Change the lyrics to accommodate other modes of transportation that have wheels.

More Curriculum Connectors

✓ Because song and lyrics are very much a part of these activities, both *music* and *language arts* are involved. *Richard Scarry's Boats* is an excellent accompaniment to these activities.

What Else I Did

_____
_____
_____
_____
_____
_____
_____
_____
_____

Traffic Lights

What It Teaches
- ✓ Traffic safety
- ✓ Color discrimination
- ✓ Motor control
- ✓ The movement element of flow

What You'll Need
Three large pieces of paper: one red, one yellow, and one green

Materials for an obstacle course (optional)

What to Do
- ✓ Talk to the children about traffic lights and what's meant by each of the three colors.
- ✓ Explain to the children that they're going to walk all around the room or playground, pretending they're driving cars. When they see you hold up the red paper, they're to come to a complete stop. When they see you hold up yellow, they should walk in place. When you hold up green, they're to walk again.

How to Ensure Success
Make sure your "traffic lights" are big enough to be seen throughout the room. Hold them high above your head.

Present the colors in the same order for a while. Once the children are experiencing success, add to the challenge by mixing up the order.

What Else You Can Do
- ✓ To enhance this game, create a "town" by decorating and/or designating certain areas of the room or playground as various locales – for example, a gas station, the grocery store, the mall, or the library. Ask the children for suggestions. Where do their parents drive them?
- ✓ Set up an obstacle course that includes objects that the "cars" must move around, over (such as bridges), and through (such as tunnels).
- ✓ Play the game using different locomotor skills.

More Curriculum Connectors
- ✓ The concept of color is central to *art*.
- ✓ Discussing traffic safety and the community relates to *language arts*. You might also share *Go! Go! Go! Stop!* by Charise Mericle Harper.

- ✓ To include *music*, play "Safety Signs" from Hap Palmer's *Learning Basic Skills Through Music: Vocabulary*.
- ✓ The concepts of over, around, and through fall under the headings of *mathematics* and *language arts*.

What Else I Did

_____
_____
_____
_____
_____
_____
_____
_____
_____

All Aboard!

What It Teaches
- ✓ Awareness of a form of transportation becoming less common
- ✓ Practice with locomotor skills
- ✓ Cooperation

What You'll Need
Masking tape or rope (optional)
Hand drum and mallet (optional)

What to Do
- ✓ Talk to the children about trains and how they are a mode of transportation for both people and products. Do they realize that trains are made up of individual cars linked together? Have they ever sat at a railroad crossing waiting for a train to go by and counted the number of cars it has?
- ✓ Explain to the children that they're each going to be individual cars of a train that have been separated from one another but are still going. They're to travel about the room or playground, moving "like trains." When they hear you say, "Choo-choo," they're to connect with one more "car." (If desired, set an appropriate beat with a drum, stopping every time you say "Choo-choo.")
- ✓ Continue the game until all the cars are linked and the train is whole once again.

How to Ensure Success
Make sure the children understand they're to link up with whichever car is *closest* to them at the time you say "Choo-choo."

Encourage the children to walk at first as they pretend to be train cars. Once they have some experience with it, suggest locomotor skills such as running or jumping.

In this activity, sound enhances the experience. Let them "chug" away!

What Else You Can Do
- ✓ Use lines you may already have on the floor, or create lines with masking tape or rope. Ask the children to imagine that the lines are narrow train tracks. Challenge them to move along the lines in various ways without "falling off." Possibilities include forward, sideward, backward, and at low and high levels. This is a great activity for balance.

More Curriculum Connectors

✓ Ask the children to count how many cars their completed train has (or count the number of cars yourself, aloud) to incorporate *mathematics*.

✓ Balance is a *science* concept.

✓ Using a drum accompaniment adds an element of *music*.

✓ Reading Donald Crew's *Freight Train* brings in *language arts* and, because it references colors, *art*.

What Else I Did

_____

_____

_____

_____

_____

_____

_____

_____

_____

By Air or By Sea

What It Teaches
- ✓ Familiarity with various modes of air and sea transportation
- ✓ Problem solving

What You'll Need
No equipment or materials needed

What to Do
- ✓ Ask the children to name and depict as many modes of transportation as they can that travel in the air or on the water.

How to Ensure Success
You may choose to have all of the discussion at once, with the children brainstorming answers. Have them stand and act out the motions of each mode of transportation, one at a time, as you call them out, or immediately follow each idea the children have with the appropriate action(s).

What Else You Can Do
- ✓ To continue with the problem solving, ask the children to think of and depict modes of transportation found primarily in cities (such as subways and taxis), that are motorless (such as hot air balloons and gliders), or that transport something other than people (such as wheelbarrows and garbage trucks).

More Curriculum Connectors
- ✓ Any discussion about transportation in which the children participate is part of *language arts*. Book possibilities include Donald Crews' *Flying*, Richard Scarry's *Cars and Trucks and Things That Go*, and Anne Rockwell's *Boats*.
- ✓ To incorporate *mathematics*, ask the children to count the number of solutions they find to each problem.

What Else I Did

_____
_____
_____
_____
_____
_____

About the Author

Rae Pica has been an education consultant (www.raepica.com) specializing in the education of the whole child, children's physical activity, and active learning since 1980. A former adjunct instructor with the University of New Hampshire, she is the author of 19 books, including the text *Experiences in Movement and Music*, in its fifth edition; the award-winning *Great Games for Young Children* and *Jump into Literacy*; and *What If Everybody Understood Child Development?: Straight Talk About Improving Education and Children's Lives*.

Known for her lively and informative keynotes and trainings, Rae also has consulted for such groups as the *Sesame Street* Research Department, the National Head Start Association, Centers for Disease Control, the President's Council on Physical Fitness and Sports, Nickelodeon's *Blues Clues*, and Gymboree, as well as for school districts and state health and WIC departments throughout the country.

Rae is cofounder of BAM Radio Network (www.bamradionetwork.com), the world's largest online education radio network, where she currently hosts *Studentcentricity: Practical Strategies for Teaching with Students at the Center*, interviewing experts in education, child development, play research, the neurosciences, and more. Additionally, she serves as an expert for NBC's Education Nation, and she hosts a YouTube channel called *Active learning with rae*.

She lives just outside Washington DC, in northern Virginia.

Made in the USA
Middletown, DE
01 July 2019